Gemma Young

Cambridge IGCSE®
Biology
Maths Skills

Workbook

First Edition

CAMBRIDGE
UNIVERSITY PRESS

CAMBRIDGE
UNIVERSITY PRESS

University Printing House, Cambridge CB2 8BS, United Kingdom

One Liberty Plaza, 20th Floor, New York, NY 10006, USA

477 Williamstown Road, Port Melbourne, VIC 3207, Australia

314–321, 3rd Floor, Plot 3, Splendor Forum, Jasola District Centre, New Delhi – 110025, India

79 Anson Road, #06–04/06, Singapore 079906

Cambridge University Press is part of the University of Cambridge.

It furthers the University's mission by disseminating knowledge in the pursuit of education, learning and research at the highest international levels of excellence.

Information on this title: www.cambridge.org

First published 2018

20 19 18 17 16 15 14 13 12 11 10 9 8 7 6 5 4 3 2 1

Printed in Spain by GraphyCems

A catalogue record for this publication is available from the British Library

ISBN 978-1-108-72812-6

Additional resources for this publication at cambridge.org/9781108728126

Cambridge University Press has no responsibility for the persistence or accuracy of URLs for external or third-party internet websites referred to in this publication, and does not guarantee that any content on such websites is, or will remain, accurate or appropriate. Information regarding prices, travel timetables, and other factual information given in this work is correct at the time of first printing but Cambridge University Press does not guarantee the accuracy of such information thereafter.

....

....

Contents

Introduction

This workbook has been written to help you to improve your skills in the mathematical processes that you need in your Cambridge IGCSE Biology course. The exercises will guide you and give you practice in:

- representing values
- working with data
- drawing graphs and charts
- interpreting data
- doing calculations
- working with shape.

Each chapter focuses on several maths skills that you need to master to be successful in your biology course. It explains why you need these skills. Then, for each skill, it presents a step-by-step worked example of a question that involves the skill. This is followed by practice questions for you to try. These are not like exam questions. They are designed to develop your skills and understanding; they get increasingly challenging. Tips are often given alongside to guide you. Spaces, lines or graph grids are provided for your answers.

In biology, there are lots of contexts where maths is used. You will be calculating magnification and using scale when working with microscopes. Probability and ratio are used to interpret the results from genetic crosses. An important skill is analysing data in the form of tables, graphs and charts. This could be data that you, or other scientists, have collected during an investigation.

There are further questions at the end of each chapter that you can try to give you more confidence in using the skills practised in the chapter. At the end of the book there are additional questions that may require any of the maths skills from all of the chapters.

Chapter 1:
Representing values

Why do you need to represent values in biology?

- In biology you will take measurements when collecting data from investigations.
- Numerical data must be recorded along with a suitable unit to give it a value so others can make sense of it.
- Often the values used are very small or very big: for example a cell might have a diameter of 0.000 01 m. Converting units or using standard notation makes it easier to understand and compare values.

Maths focus 1: Using units

A biologist measured the length and mass of the fish in Figure 1.1.

She wrote down the measurements as 64 cm and 10.9 kg.

Figure 1.1 A type of fish called a 'carp'

When taking measurements in biology it is important to choose a suitable **unit**.

The measuring apparatus you use can help you decide what units to use. The biologist used a tape measure that measured length in centimetres and weighing scales that measured mass in kilograms.

It is also correct to say that the fish has a length of 0.00064 km and a mass of 10 900 g, but these units were not chosen because the numbers are either very small or very large. This makes it harder to understand them.

What maths skills do you need to be able to use units?

1	Choosing the correct unit	• Consider what measuring apparatus is being used and what it measures
		• Choose the most suitable unit
2	Using unit symbols	• Decide what the unit is
		• Write the correct symbol
3	Using derived units	• Identify the units being used
		• Decide what the calculation is
		• Work out the derived unit

Maths skill practice

How does using units relate to practical work in biology?

When doing practical work in biology you will use apparatus to make measurements and collect data. It is important that you record this data using an appropriate unit.

For example, if you measure the length of a leaf and record it as 5, it is not clear whether you mean 5 millimetres or 5 centimetres. This difference in length is significant and will mean that your results cannot be interpreted correctly.

Maths skill 1: Choosing the correct unit

Table 1.1 shows some of the measurements commonly used in biology, along with the apparatus used to measure them and the units they can be measured in.

Measurement	Apparatus	Unit
length/width	ruler	millimetres
	tape measure	centimetres
		metres
mass	weighing scales	grams
		kilograms
volume	measuring cylinder	cubic centimetres
	pipette	
temperature	thermometer	degrees Celsius
time	stop clock	seconds

Table 1.1 Common measurements and apparatus used in biology

WORKED EXAMPLE 1

A student investigates transpiration using a potometer. Figure 1.2 shows the apparatus she uses.

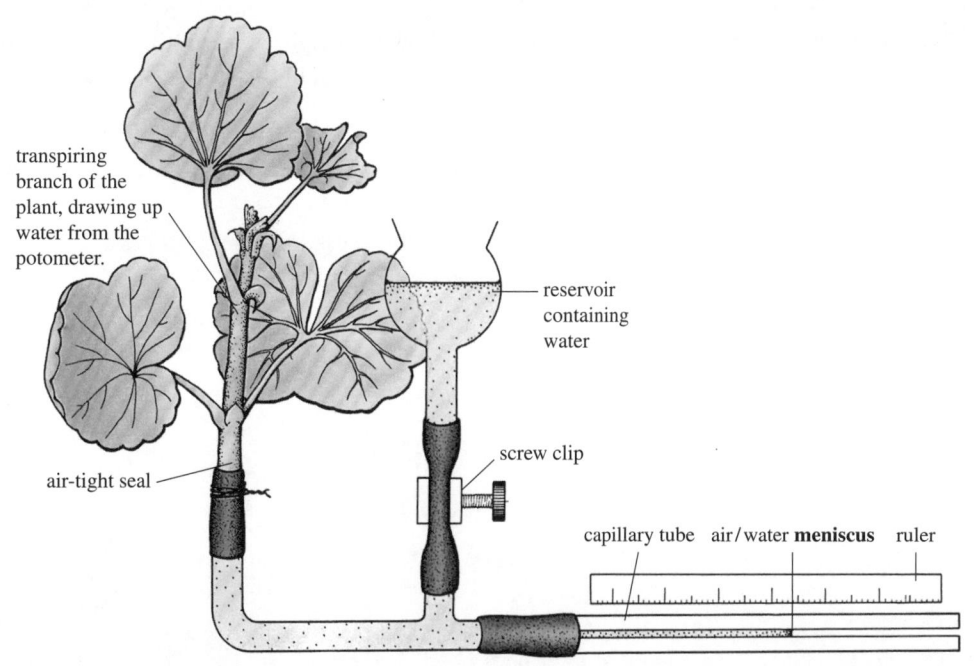

transpiring branch of the plant, drawing up water from the potometer.

reservoir containing water

air-tight seal

screw clip

capillary tube   air/water **meniscus**   ruler

Figure 1.2 A potometer

3

TIP

Choose a unit that will give you numbers that are not too small or not too large.

She measures the distance the meniscus moves in 5 minutes using the ruler, which has divisions in both centimetres and millimetres.

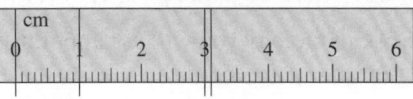

1 centimetre   1 millimetre

Figure 1.3 A ruler divided into millimetres and centimetres

Which unit should she use to measure the distance?

> **KEY QUESTIONS TO ASK YOURSELF:**
>
> - What measuring apparatus is being used?
> - What is it measuring?
> - What are the units of the divisions on it?
> - Which unit is the most appropriate to use?

The student should use millimetres. She could also use centimetres, although this would mean her data contains a decimal point.

It would be a mistake to use metres as the unit because the values would be too small.

WATCH OUT

Make sure you use the correct *case* for the letters in the symbols. For example, cm is written in lower case letters, but °C is an upper case letter. Other units, for example kJ (kilojoules) contain both.

Practice question 1

A biologist is investigating variation in physical characteristics in humans.

He asks a person to step onto some scales.

a What measurement is he taking? ....

b What unit would be most appropriate to use? ....

Practice question 2

A student investigates how the height of a seedling changes over time. She decides to measure the height in kilometres. Why would this not be a good choice of unit to measure the height?

....

Suggest a suitable unit. ....

4

Maths skill 2: Using unit symbols

Instead of writing out the unit name each time, you can use a shorter version called a **symbol** (see Table 1.2).

Unit	Symbol
metre	m
centimetre	cm
millimetre	mm
kilogram	kg
gram	g
degrees Celsius	°C
cubic centimetre	cm^3
second	s

Table 1.2 Some units and their symbols

WORKED EXAMPLE 2

A student did an osmosis experiment. They cut up a potato into small cubes with sides of equal length. They then placed the cubes into test tubes containing the same amount of pure water.

What measurements did they take in setting up the experiment? What units should they use for each?

Length of sides of potato cube. They should use mm.

Volume of salt solution. They should use cm^3.

Practice question 3

Using Table 1.2, write down the unit symbol that would be used for each of the following measurements:

a volume of water measured using a pipette ....

b thickness of a leaf ....

c temperature of the room ....

d time taken for an enzyme to break down a substrate ....

5

TIP

The / symbol indicates a division. When reading aloud derived units, say the / as 'per'. For example, g/cm^3 is said as 'grams per cubic centimetre'.

TIP

g/cm^3 can also be written as $g\,cm^{-3}$. They both mean the same thing.

Maths skill 3: Using derived units

Some units are made up (**derived**) from other units.

Concentration of a solution can be measured in g/cm^3. This unit came from a calculation. To calculate concentration you divide mass by volume:

$$concentration = \frac{mass}{volume}$$

so the units are g/cm^3.

WORKED EXAMPLE 3

A scientist used a microscope to study pollen tubes growing.

A pollen tube grew 2.4 mm in 600 seconds.

What unit should you use to show the rate of growth?

mm/s

(So, the rate of growth was $\frac{2.4}{600} = 0.004\ mm/s$)

Practice question 4

For each measurement being described, write down the derived unit.

a   A quantity of sugar in grams was dissolved in a volume of water measured in cubic centimetres (cm^3). ....

b   A cat ran across a room. The time taken was measured in seconds.

....

Practice question 5

A student investigates an enzyme-catalysed reaction.

He adds an enzyme to a substrate and measures the volume of product made over a period of time.

Identify the derived unit he would use to present his data. ....

Maths focus 2: Representing very large and very small values

In biology you often have to use very small or large numbers.

For example:

• The diameter of a strand of DNA is 0.000 000 004 m.

• There are around 37 200 000 000 000 cells in the human body.

Values written like this are hard to understand and it is easy to make a mistake and include incorrect numbers or miss some out.

Also, writing them takes a long time, and a lot of space.

For these reasons biologists often use **standard form**.

Converting the values into standard form gives us:

- The diameter of a strand of DNA is 4×10^{-9} m.

- There are around 3.72×10^{13} cells in the human body.

These numbers are shorter and clearer. It also makes it easier to compare the size of the numbers.

What maths skills do you need to represent very small and very large numbers?

1	Writing very large numbers in standard form	• Write the number as a number between 1 and 10, e.g. 900 is written as 9
		• Count how many times the number has to be multiplied by 10, e.g. $900 = 9 \times 10 \times 10$ so it has to be multiplied by 10 twice
		• Then convert the multiple of 10 to a power of 10, e.g. $9 \times 10 \times 10 = 9 \times 10^2$
2	Writing very small numbers in standard form	• Write the number as a number between 1 and 9, e.g. 0.05 is written as 5
		• Count how many times the number has to be divided by 10, e.g. $0.05 = 5 \div 10 \div 10$ so it has to be divided by 10 twice
		• Then convert the multiple of 10 to a power of 10, e.g. $5 \div 10 \div 10 = 5 \times 10^{-2}$

Maths skill 1: Writing very large numbers in standard form

WORKED EXAMPLE 4

Convert the number 30 000 into standard form.

Step 1: Write the number as a number between 1 and 10.

For this number it is 3.

Step 2: Count how many times the number has to be multiplied by 10 to get the original number.

To convert the number 3 to 30 000 it has to be multiplied by 10 four times.

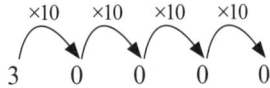

$$3 \quad 0 \quad 0 \quad 0 \quad 0$$

Step 3: Convert the multiple of 10 to a power of 10.

$$3 \times 10^4 \quad \longleftarrow \quad \text{The 4 shows that we had to multiply 3 by 10 four times.}$$

The number is now in standard form.

TIP

Using standard form makes it easier to compare the size of numbers.

For example, it is clear that 2.6×10^5 is around 100 bigger than 2.2×10^3.

Practice question 6

Convert these numbers to standard form.

a 50 000 ....

b 6700 ....

c 275 000 000 ....

Practice question 7

Convert these numbers from standard form:

a 2.08×10^2 ....

b 9.25×10^5 ....

c 1.006×10^8 ....

Practice question 8

A colony of bacteria contains 17 000 000 bacteria.

Write this number in standard form. ....

Maths skill 2: Writing very small numbers in standard form

TIP

In standard form the decimal point is always placed after the first non-zero figure.

TIP

When transforming numbers less than 1 into standard form you use a negative number for the power.

WORKED EXAMPLE 5

Convert the number 0.000 075 into standard form.

Step 1: Write the number as a number between 1 and 10.

For this number it is 7.5.

Step 2: Count how many times the number has to be divided by 10.

To convert the number 7.5 to 0.000 075, it has to be divided by 10 five times.

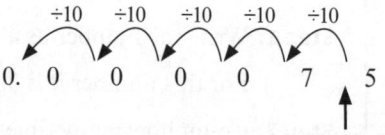

$$\begin{array}{ccccccc} & \div 10 & \div 10 & \div 10 & \div 10 & \div 10 \\ 0. & 0 & 0 & 0 & 0 & 7 & 5 \end{array}$$

The decimal point was here

Step 3: Convert the multiple of 10 to a power of 10.

$$7.5 \times 10^{-5}$$

The −5 shows that we had to divide 7.5 by 10 five times

The number is now in standard form.

Practice question 9

Convert these numbers to standard form.

a 0.003 ....

b 0.000 060 8 ....

c 0.000 000 041 08 ....

Practice question 10

Convert these numbers from standard form:

a 6×10^{-4} ....

b 7.22×10^{-7} ....

c 5.008×10^{-3} ....

Practice question 11

The **diameter** of an animal cell is 0.000 105 m.

Write this in standard form. ....

Maths focus 3: Using unit prefixes and converting units

When you measure mass at school you will normally use the unit *grams*.

However, grams are not an appropriate unit to measure the mass of much smaller or larger objects. Here are the masses of two animals:

$$\text{Mass of a mosquito} = 0.0025\,\text{g}$$

$$\text{Mass of a giant tortoise} = 200\,000\,\text{g}$$

You can add a **unit prefix** to the start of a unit to change its value.

For example, the prefix *kilo-* makes the unit *one thousand times larger*. So:

$$1\,\text{kg} = 1000\,\text{g}$$

The prefix *milli-* makes the unit *one thousand times smaller*. So:

$$1\,\text{mg} = 0.001\,\text{g}$$

You can use these to convert the masses of the animals to a more appropriate unit:

$$\text{Mass of a mosquito} = 2.5\,\text{mg}$$

$$\text{Mass of a giant tortoise} = 200\,\text{kg}$$

What maths skills do you need to use unit prefixes and convert units?

1	Using powers of ten	• Write powers of tens as numbers
		• Write numbers as powers of ten
2	Using negative powers of ten	• Write negative powers of tens as numbers
		• Write numbers as negative powers of ten
3	Using unit prefixes	• Convert the number into a power of ten
4	Converting units	• Decide if you need to multiply or divide
		• Do the calculation. Make sure you add units to your answer
		• Check that the size of the answer looks correct

Maths skill 1: Using powers of ten

You already know that 10^2 can be read as '10 squared' and means 10×10. Its value is 100.

This can also be read as '10 to the power of 2'.

The small number is the **power** or **index**. It shows how many times we multiply by 10; see Table 1.3.

Power of 10	Multiplying tens	Value	Name
10^0	–	1	one
10^1	10	10	ten
10^2	10×10	100	one hundred
10^3	$10 \times 10 \times 10$	1000	one thousand
10^4	$10 \times 10 \times 10 \times 10$	10000	ten thousand
10^5			
10^6			

Table 1.3 Some powers of 10 and their values

TIP

The number of zeros in the value is the same as the power. So 10^2 is 100, which shows that 1 has been multiplied by 10 two times.

TIP

Leaving a space between every three digits makes larger numbers easier to read. For example, one million written as 1 000 000 is more easily recognised than 1000000.

10

WORKED EXAMPLE 6

Explain why 1000 can also be written as 10^3

1000 = 10 × 10 × 10

So, 10 is multiplied by itself 3 times

This can be written as 10^3

Practice question 12

Complete the final two rows of Table 1.3.

Practice question 13

Write the following as powers of 10:

a 1000 ....

b 1 000 000 000 ....

c 10 million ....

Practice question 14

Write the values of the following powers of 10:

a 10^5 ....

b 10^8 ....

c 10^{10} ....

Maths skill 2: Using negative powers of ten

Powers of ten can also have negative values.

Table 1.4 shows how these are calculated.

Power of 10	Dividing tens	Value	Name
10^{-1}	$1 \div 10$	0.1	one tenth
10^{-2}	$1 \div (10 \times 10)$	0.01	one hundredth
10^{-5}	$1 \div (10 \times 10 \times 10 \times 10 \times 10)$	0.00001	one hundred thousandth
10^{-6}	$1 \div (10 \times 10 \times 10 \times 10 \times 10 \times 10)$	0.000001	one millionth

Table 1.4 Calculating negative powers of ten

The negative index or power of 10 tells you how many times to divide by 10.

$$10^{-2} \text{ is } \frac{1}{10 \times 10} = \frac{1}{100}$$

$$10^{-5} \text{ is } \frac{1}{10 \times 10 \times 10 \times 10 \times 10} = \frac{1}{100\,000}$$

WORKED EXAMPLE 7

Explain why 0.01 can also be written as 10^{-2}

0.01 = 10 ÷ 10 ÷ 10

So, 10 is divided by itself twice

This can be written as 10^{-2}

Practice question 15

Complete the missing two rows of Table 1.4.

Practice question 16

Write the following as powers of 10:

a 0.01 ....

b 0.000 000 000 1 ....

c one ten millionth ....

Practice question 17

Write the values of the following powers of 10:

a 10^{-1} ....

b 10^{-4} ....

c 10^{-8} ....

Maths skill 3: Using unit prefixes

A prefix is added to the start of a unit to change its value.

Each prefix has a **power of ten** associated with it.

Table 1.5 shows the prefixes most commonly used in biology.

WATCH OUT

The symbol for the prefix micro- might look like a u in some print, but it is in fact a Greek letter (called *mu*). Make sure you write it correctly.

Prefix	Prefix symbol	Power of ten	Example	
			Unit name	Unit symbol
kilo-	k	10^3	kilometre	km
–	–	10^0	metre	m
deci-	d	10^{-1}	decimetre	dm
centi-	c	10^{-2}	centimetre	cm
milli-	m	10^{-3}	millimetre	mm
micro-	μ	10^{-6}	micrometre	μm
nano-	n	10^{-9}	nanometre	nm

Table 1.5 Common prefixes used in biology

WORKED EXAMPLE 8

The length of a bacterial cell is 0.000 001 m.

This value is better displayed either by using **standard notation** or by using a unit with a prefix.

$$0.000\,001 = 1 \times 10^{-6}$$

so

$$0.000\,001\,\text{m} = 1 \times 10^{-6}\,\text{m} = 1\,\mu\text{m}.$$

Practice question 18

Write the missing unit symbol.

The first has been done has an example.

a $10^3\,\text{m} = 1\,\text{km}$

b $10^3\,\text{g} = 1$ ....

c $10^{-2}\,\text{m}^3 = 1$ ....

d $10^{-3}\,\text{s} = 1$ ....

e $10^{-9}\,\text{J} = 1$ ....

Practice question 19

A cell membrane is 0.000 000 01 m thick.

Write this number down using a more appropriate unit.

....

....

....

Maths skill 4: Converting units

If you convert data so it is all in the same unit, it will be easier to compare.

For example, two objects have the masses 0.45 g and 900 mg. Converting both to milligrams will give you the values 450 mg and 900 mg, so you can see that the second mass is double the first.

Table 1.6 shows you how to convert units.

Prefix	Example	Power of ten
kilo-	kg	10^3
–	g	10^0
milli-	mg	10^{-3}
micro-	µg	10^{-6}
nano-	ng	10^{-9}

÷ 1000 (left side, repeated between rows) × 1000 (right side, repeated between rows)

Table 1.6 Converting units

TIP

Check your answer by looking at its size. For example, you know that microgram (µg) is a smaller unit than gram (g), so it makes sense that 10 µg would be a small number when converted into grams.

WORKED EXAMPLE 9

Convert 10 µg into grams.

To convert µg to g you need to divide the number by 1000 twice (1000²).

$$\frac{10}{1000^2} = 0.00001 \text{ g}$$

Practice question 20

Convert the following numbers:

a 1 m into millimetres

....

b 14 g into kilograms

....

c 1200 µm into millimetres

....

Practice question 21

The diameter of a red blood cell is 8 µm. Convert this into millimetres.

....

Further questions

1 **a** A student investigated how caffeine found in an energy drink affected her reaction time. The energy drink she decided to use contains 80 mg of caffeine in a 250 cm³ can.

Calculate the amount of caffeine in the drink in mg/cm³.

....

....

b The student measured her reaction time five times before drinking the energy drink.

To get accurate results she used a computer program to do this.

Her results were:

        0.315 s   0.423 s   0.345 s   0.478 s   0.278 s

i Calculate her mean reaction time in seconds.

....

....

ii Convert this time to milliseconds.

....

....

   c Next, she needed to drink a cup of the energy drink.

      Suggest a suitable unit for measuring the volume of energy drink.

      Explain why you chose this unit.

      ....

      ....

   d She then waited 10 minutes before repeating the reaction time test.

      Her mean reaction time was lower than it was before she drank the energy drink.

      What conclusion can she make from this evidence?

      ....

2 A scientist counted 9856 white blood cells in $1\,\mu l$ of blood.

  Calculate an estimate for the number of white blood cells in 5 litres of blood (the average volume of blood in an adult man).

  ....

  ....

  Write the answer in standard form.

  ....

Chapter 2:
Working with data

Why do you need to work with data in biology?

- In biology you will do many investigations and gather data as evidence.
- Data must be collected accurately, reducing the number of errors.
- Data are usually recorded in a results table. This allows you to see patterns more clearly in the data so you can draw conclusions.

Maths focus 1: Naming types of data

Whenever an investigation is carried out in biology, variables (factors that can be measured, controlled or changed) are used. One variable is chosen to be changed. This is the **independent variable**.

One variable will be measured. This is the **dependent variable**. This is recorded in the results table.

All the other variables are kept the same. This ensures that the test is fair. These are **control variables**.

Data may be recorded as words, or as numbers. Data recorded as words is **categorical data**. Examples of categorical data include eye colour, type of plant. If the data are recorded as numbers and the numbers take only certain values, such as shoe size, this is categorical data.

- **Categorical data** – where the data can be sorted into categories (groups) but the categories cannot be easily ordered, e.g. the names of animals

- **Continuous data** – where the data can take any value within a certain range, e.g. the temperature of an object

- **Discrete data** – where the data can only take certain values, the number of petals on a flower can only be whole numbers.

Naming the types of data will help you to decide how to arrange the data in a results table and also what type of chart or graph to use to display the data.

What maths skills do you need when naming types of data?

1	Identifying independent and dependent variables	•	Identify the variable that is changed – this is the independent variable
		•	Identify the variable that is measured – this is the dependent variable
2	Identifying types of data	•	Decide if the data are recorded as words or not; if the data are words, then these are categorical data
		•	If the data are recorded as numbers, decide if the data can take any value. If it can, these are continuous data; if it can only take certain values, these are discrete data

Maths skills practice

How does identifying types of data relate to displaying data in biology?

Data can be displayed in a results table.

The independent variable goes in the first column and the dependent variable goes in the second column:

Name of independent variable goes here	Name of dependent variable goes here

LINK

See Maths focus 3, 'Recording and processing data', to learn more about how to record data in tables.

When drawing a chart or graph the independent variable goes on the horizontal (*x*-axis), and the dependent variable goes on the vertical (*y*-axis); see Figure 2.1.

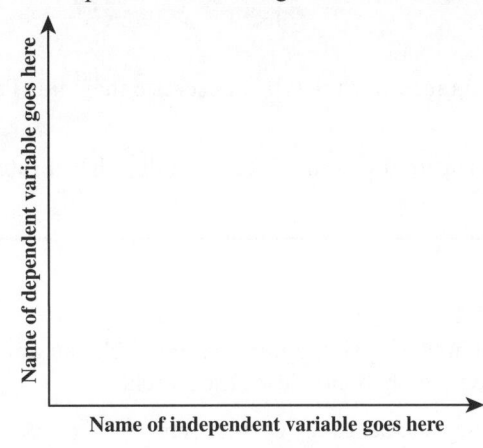

Figure 2.1 How to plot the variables on a graph

Whether the data are categorical, discrete or continuous will help you to decide what type of chart or graph to draw.

- If the independent variable is *categorical* or *discrete* then you should use a **bar chart**.
- If the independent variable is *continuous* then you should use a **line graph**.

LINK

You can find out more about drawing charts and graphs in Chapter 3, 'Drawing graphs and charts'.

Maths skill 1: Identifying independent and dependent variables

WATCH OUT

The variable you *change* is called the *independent* variable. The variable you *measure* is called the *dependent* variable.

WORKED EXAMPLE 1

Two students carried out an investigation to see how different types of exercise affected heart rate.

They ran on the spot, skipped and did star jumps for 1 minute. They measured the increase in their heart rate in beats per minute.

What variables did they use?

KEY QUESTIONS TO ASK YOURSELF:

- What variable did they change? This is the *independent* variable.

- What variable did they measure? This is the *dependent* variable.

The variable they changed was the type of exercise they did. This is the independent variable.

The variable they measured was the increase in their heart rate. This is the dependent variable.

Practice question 1

A student investigated how the pH of a mixture of starch and amylase affected how long it took the amylase to completely break down the starch.

Draw lines to match the variable to the correct type.

Temperature of mixture   Independent variable

pH of mixture   Dependent variable

Time taken to break down the starch   Control variable (variable they kept the same)

Practice question 2

State the independent and dependent variable used in each of these investigations:

a Studying the number of measles cases in the USA every year over the last 100 years.

....

b Measuring the change in mass of pieces of potato left in salt solutions with different concentrations.

....

c Counting the number of dandelion plants growing in areas with different light intensities.

....

Maths skill 2: Identifying types of data

WORKED EXAMPLE 2

Table 2.1 shows data on the effectiveness of different types of contraception in a western country in a sample of 100 women.

Contraception method	Percentage of women becoming pregnant in the first year/ %
none	85
diaphragm	40
condom	14
oral contraceptive	0

Table 2.1 Effectiveness of contraception

What type of data are shown in Table 2.1?

KEY QUESTIONS TO ASK YOURSELF:

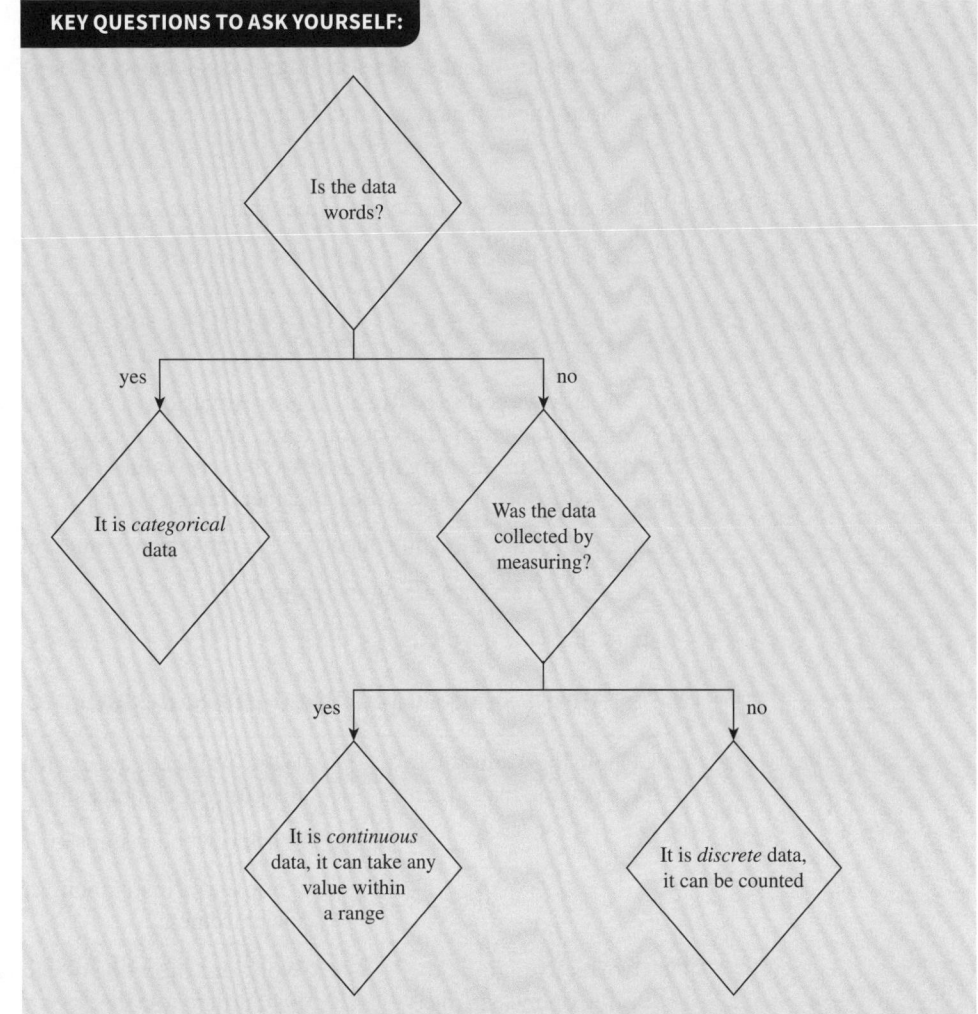

In this example the independent variable is the type of contraception. The variable is provided as words, so these are categorical data.

The dependent variable is the percentage of women. The data are numbers, but were not collected by measuring so these are discrete data.

Practice question 3

A scientist collected data on trees in a forest.

State if each of the following are categorical, continuous or discrete data.

a   Number of trees in the forest ....

b   Height of tree ....

c   Species of tree ....

d   Number of leaves on a branch ....

e   Width of leaf ....

f   Colour of flowers ....

Practice question 4

A student investigated how a variable affected the growth of cress seedlings.

This is the method she followed:

1   Place five cress seeds on cotton wool in four different Petri dishes.

2   Add a different volume of water to each dish every day.

3   Measure the height of the seedlings every 2 days for 2 weeks.

   a   State the independent and dependent variables.

   ....

   b   State if each of these are categorical, continuous or discrete data. Explain how
       you decided.

   ....

Maths focus 2: Collecting data

Data are always collected during an investigation in biology and data *quality* is important.
If errors are made when collecting data, the results will not be accurate. These errors would
give data that are that are not close to the true values. The difference between the true value
and the value measured is called the **uncertainty**.

To make sure the data you collect are accurate you should make sure you:

• use the correct measuring instrument

• read the scale correctly.

What maths skills do you need to record and process data?

1	Choosing a suitable measuring instrument	• Work out the maximum and minimum values each instrument can measure
		• Work out the resolution
		• Choose the instrument that will give the most accurate measurement
2	Correctly reading the value on measuring instruments	• Work out the value of each individual mark on the instrument's scale
		• When using a measuring cylinder, view the level of the liquid at eye level and record the volume from the bottom of the meniscus
3	Using the correct number of significant figures	• Make sure the measurement has the same number of **decimal places** as the resolution of the measuring equipment

Maths skill practice

How does recording and processing data help?

Figure 2.2 and Table 2.2 show some of the measuring instruments you often use in biology.

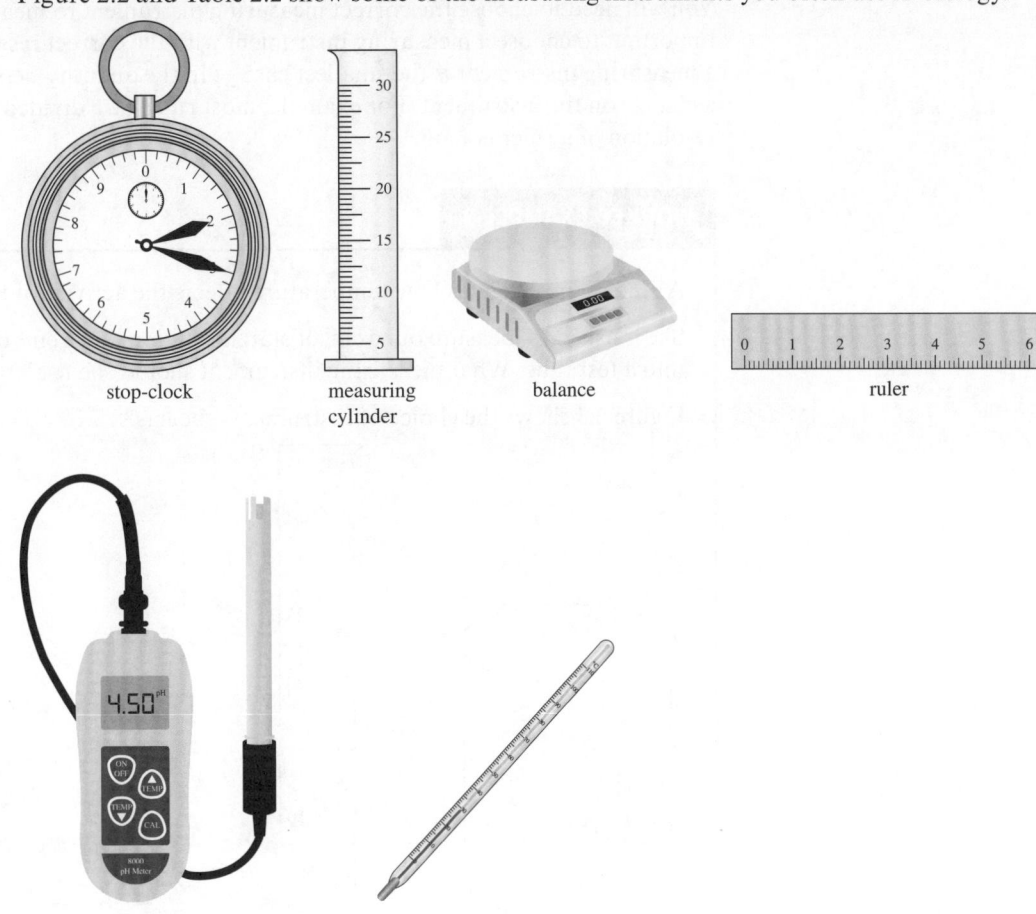

stop-clock   measuring cylinder   balance   ruler

pH probe   thermometer

Figure 2.2 Different types of measuring instruments used in biology

Instrument	What it measures	Unit(s) used
stop-clock	time	seconds (s)
measuring cylinder	volume	cubic centimetres (cm³)
balance	mass	grams (g)
ruler	length	centimetres (cm), millimetres (mm)
pH probe	pH	–
thermometer	temperature	degrees Celsius (°C)

Table 2.2 What the instruments measure and the units used

Maths skill 1: Choosing a suitable measuring instrument

When you are planning an investigation, you will decide on your dependent variable and what you will need to measure.

You will need to choose the correct measuring instrument to measure this variable. It is important to choose a measuring instrument with the correct **resolution**. The resolution of a measuring instrument is the smallest change in the quantity being measured that gives a change on the instrument. For example, most rulers are divided into millimetres so the resolution of a ruler is 1 mm.

WORKED EXAMPLE 3

A student investigates how temperature affects the activity of the enzyme amylase.

She is asked to measure out 5 cm³ of starch solution and 1 cm³ of amylase and place this into a test tube. What measuring instrument should she use?

Figure 2.3 shows the choice of instruments she has.

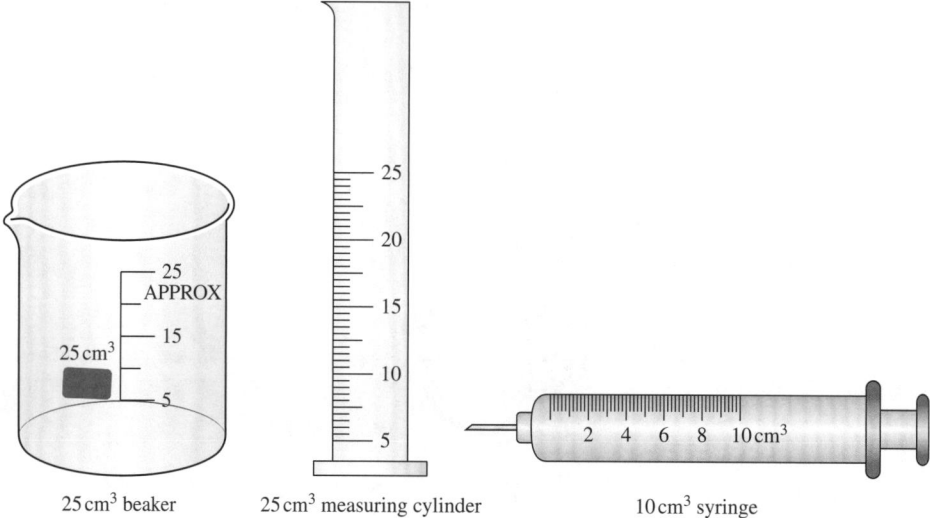

25 cm³ beaker   25 cm³ measuring cylinder   10 cm³ syringe

Figure 2.3 Measuring instruments used to measure liquids

KEY QUESTIONS TO ASK YOURSELF:

- What is the minimum and maximum volume each instrument can measure?
- What is the resolution of each instrument?
- Which instrument will give the most accurate measurement?

LINK

See Maths skill 2, 'Correctly reading the value on measuring instruments', to learn more about how to measure accurately.

TIP

When measuring small volumes you should use a small measuring cylinder or a syringe. These will give you the most accurate measurements.

The beaker would not be a good choice because measuring such small volumes in it would not be very accurate. The markings on the side go up by $5\,cm^3$ each time, so its resolution is $5\,cm^3$. You could only measure a volume accurately to the nearest $5\,cm^3$ – so it could not be used to measure out $1\,cm^3$ accurately as the uncertainty of the measurement would be high. For this reason, beakers are only used to measure rough volumes.

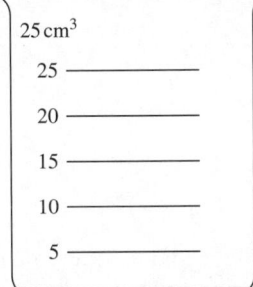

Figure 2.4 Does this beaker contain $1\,cm^3$?

If you use this beaker to try to measure $1\,cm^3$, your measurement will not be very accurate – it will have a high uncertainty.

The measuring cylinder measures the same volume as the beaker, but it has a higher resolution ($0.5\,cm^3$). It will give a more accurate measurement, as long as it is used properly.

The best choice would be the syringe. This has a resolution of 0.2 cm3, and so would give the most accurate measurement for small volumes.

23

Practice question 5

Which of the following instruments would be the best choice to measure $17\,cm^3$ of water?

Give a reason for your answer.

A a $15\,cm^3$ measuring cylinder

B a $25\,cm^3$ beaker

C a $25\,cm^3$ measuring cylinder

D a $50\,cm^3$ measuring cylinder

....

Practice question 6

Figure 2.5 shows a ruler.

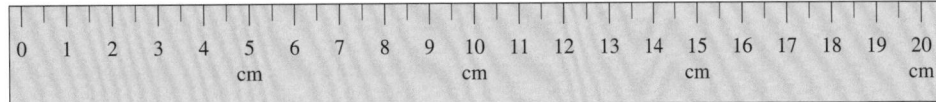

Figure 2.5 A ruler

a What is the maximum length it can measure? ....

b What is its resolution? ....

c Explain why a ruler that measures in millimetres will give a more accurate measurement. ....

Maths skill 2: Correctly reading the value on measuring instruments

Some measuring instruments are digital, for example an electronic balance or a pH probe. These instruments give you a value that you can easily read from a screen, see Figure 2.6.

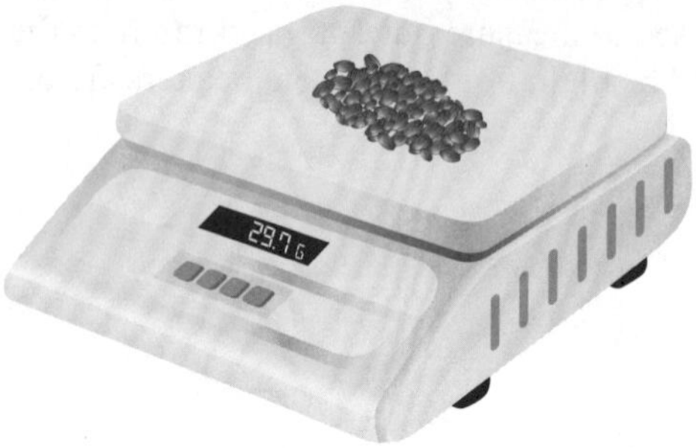

Figure 2.6 This balance has a resolution of 0.1 g

Other measuring instruments are analogue and have a scale on them which you use to read the value of the variable you are measuring, such as a thermometer and a ruler. It is more difficult to read analogue instruments than digital, as you have to judge the value by eye.

WATCH OUT

Sometimes, the level of the liquid is in between two of the lines.

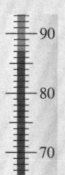

Figure 2.8 Reading the temperature when the level of the liquid does not lie exactly on a line

The level is half-way between 86 °C and 87 °C.

The temperature is 86.5 °C.

Because the level of the liquid is not exactly on a line the reading is an **estimate**. The actual temperature could be closer to 86.4 °C or 86.6 °C.

WORKED EXAMPLE 4

Mercury thermometers are analogue measuring instruments.

They have a scale which you have to read in order to work out the temperature that is being measured.

Step 1   Work out the scale on the thermometer.

KEY QUESTIONS TO ASK YOURSELF:

- What is the value between each division on the scale?
- What is the value of each line between the numbers on the scale?
- What is the reading?

Step 2   Read the value at the top of the liquid thread.

Figure 2.7 Reading the temperature on a thermometer

On this thermometer, the value between each division is 10. The scale shows 0 °C, 10 °C, 20 °C, 30 °C.

There are 10 lines between each number. Therefore, the value of each line is $\frac{10}{10} = 1$ °C.

The liquid in the thermometer has reached one line above 20 °C.

The temperature must be: 20 + 1 = 21 °C

Care must be taken when measuring the volume of liquids. A student uses a measuring cylinder to measure out 25 cm³ of water, as shown in Figure 2.9.

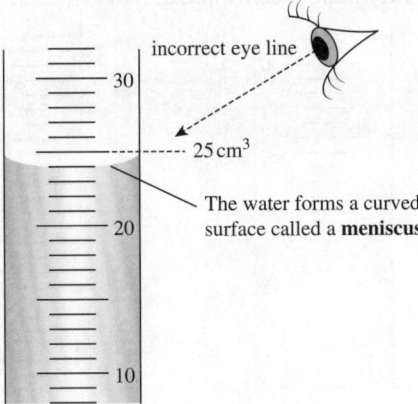

Figure 2.9 Incorrectly measuring 25 cm³ of water

The student looks down at the level of the water and it looks like the level of the water is at 25 cm³, but it is actually 24 cm³.

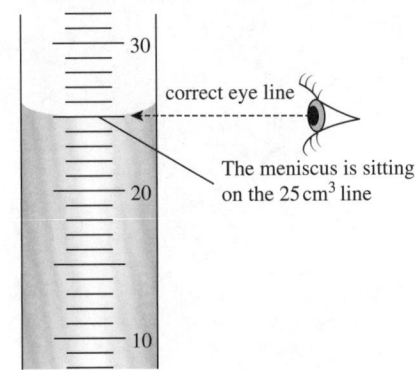

Figure 2.10 How you should measure 25 cm³ of water

Practice question 7

State the temperature reading on each thermometer.

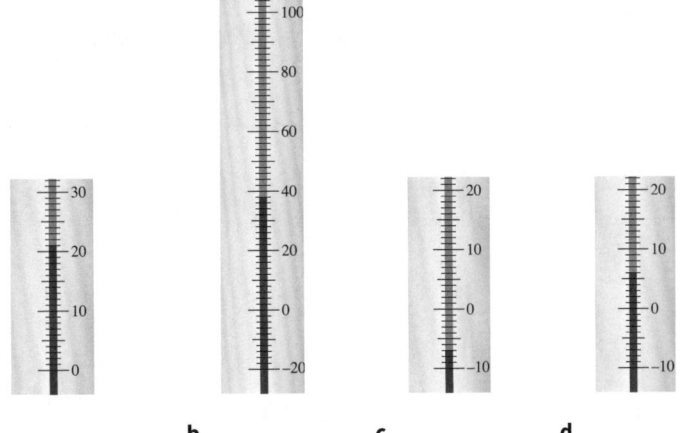

a ....   b ....   c ....   d ....

25

Practice question 8

State the volume of the liquid in cubic centimetres (cm³) in each measuring cylinder.

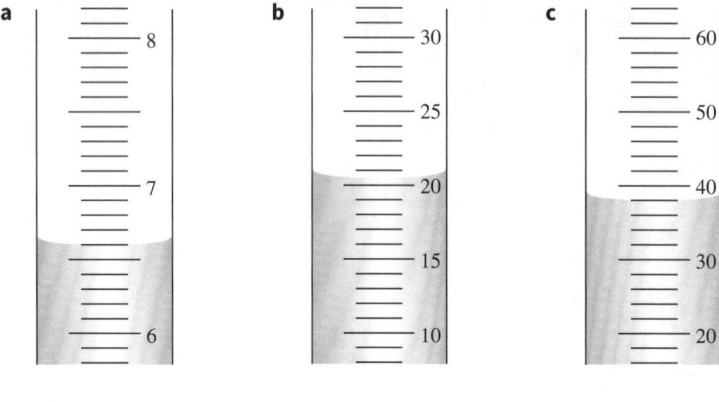

....

Practice question 9

Figure 2.11 shows a scientist with a volume of a liquid she would like to measure.

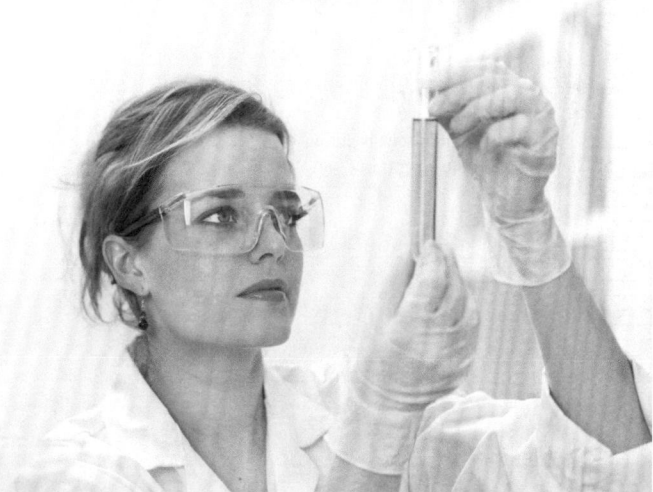

Figure 2.11 A volume of liquid to be measured

She decides to use a measuring cylinder. Explain what she should do to make sure her measurement is accurate.

....

....

....

Maths skill 3: Using the correct number of significant figures

Figure 2.12 shows how a student uses a ruler to measure the length of a leaf.

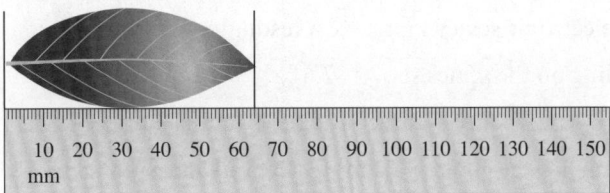

Figure 2.12 Measuring the length of a leaf

She writes down the length as 64 mm. She cannot use this ruler to measure the length to a higher **precision**, for example 64.4 mm, because it is difficult to judge fractions of a millimetre on a ruler.

64 mm is given to two significant figures. This means that the true length of the leaf is not *exactly* 64 mm but it is more likely to be close to 64 mm than to 63 mm or 65 mm.

She could have also written down the length as 6.4 cm or 0.064 m. Both these answers are also to two **significant figures**.

She then uses the same ruler to measure the length of another leaf. The length is 101 mm. This time the length is given to three significant figures.

There are some rules to counting the number of significant figures:

- Non-zero numbers are always included, e.g. 26.7 has three significant figures.

- Any zeros in between non-zero numbers are included, e.g. 4057 has four significant figures.

- If there are zeros in between a decimal point and a non-zero number, these are not included, e.g. 0.005 has one significant figure *but* any zeros after the non-zero number are included, e.g. 0.005 00 and 3.00 both have three significant figures.

WORKED EXAMPLE 5

The student then uses digital scales to measure the mass of the leaves.

The scales have a resolution of 0.01 g. Figure 2.13 shows the display on the scales.

a   `1.22 g`   b   `3.00 g`

Figure 2.13 The mass of each leaf is measured using electronic scales

She writes down the masses as 1.22 g and 3 g.

What has she done wrong?

She should have recorded the mass of the second leaf as 3.00 g (so both numbers are to three significant figures). Writing 3 g indicates that the scales only have a resolution of 1 g.

Practice question 10

State the number of significant figures in each of these numbers:

a   23 ....

b   101 ....

c   4.568 ....

d   0.06 ....

e   0.1005 ....

f   1.0038 ....

Practice question 11

A student measures his body mass.

He uses electronic scales that have a resolution of 0.1 kg.

The reading on the scales shows 82.6 kg.

a State the number of significant figures in this number. ....

b Explain how he could get a more accurate measurement of his mass.

....

c Describe how the number of significant figures in the measurement would change.

....

Maths focus 3: Recording and processing data

When you do an investigation in biology you will collect data. This could be done by counting and/or making measurements.

It is important to record the data you collect in a table. This will help you to see patterns in the data so you can work out the relationship between the variables.

What maths skills do you need to record and process data?

1	Designing a suitable results table	• Write the name of the independent variable in the first column; include the units used to measure it
		• Write the name of the dependent variable in the second column; include units
		• If you used repeats, include more than one column for the dependent variable and include a column for the mean
		• Add a row for each value you used for the independent variable
2	Calculating the mean	• Spot **outliers** (values that are much larger or smaller than the other values)
		• Add together the repeats (not including any outliers)
		• Divide the total by the number of readings
		• Use the correct number of significant figures in the answer

Maths skill practice

How does recording data in a table help in an investigation of respiration rate?

The word equation for aerobic respiration is:

$$glucose + oxygen \rightarrow carbon\ dioxide + water$$

The rate of respiration can be measured by measuring the volume of carbon dioxide produced over a time period, such as 2 minutes. The higher the volume of carbon dioxide produced, the faster the rate of respiration.

Figure 2.14 shows the equipment that can be used to investigate how temperature affects the rate of aerobic respiration in yeast.

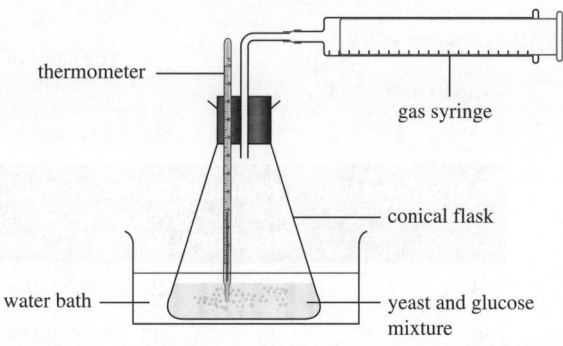

Figure 2.14 Equipment used to measure the rate of respiration in yeast. The water bath is used to change the temperature of the yeast mixture; the volume of carbon dioxide produced in 2 minutes by the yeast is measured using the gas syringe

The volume of carbon dioxide produced at each temperature is measured more than once, usually three times. A **mean** is then calculated. Repeating measurements increases the **accuracy** of the results because calculating a mean evens out the effects of errors. It also allows you to see any unusual results.

Due to the volume of data collected, it is important to record it in a results table.

Maths skill 1: Designing a suitable results table

LINK

Refer to Maths skills 2, 'Calculating the mean', to learn more about unusual results.

29

WORKED EXAMPLE 6

A student investigates how temperature affected the rate of aerobic respiration in yeast using the equipment shown in Figure 2.14.

She repeats each temperature three times and writes down the results after each measurement, as shown in Figure 2.15.

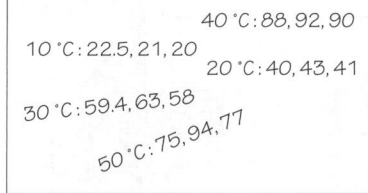

Figure 2.15 A student's results

If someone else saw the student's results, they would find it difficult to understand what the data mean. Also it is hard for her to work out any patterns in the results and draw conclusions from this data.

Therefore, she decides to put the data into a results table. How should she do this?

KEY QUESTIONS TO ASK YOURSELF:

- What is the independent variable? What unit is used to measure it?

- What is the dependent variable? What unit is used to measure it?

- How many different values for the independent variable did she use? (This is the **range**.)

- How many repeats did she make?

TIP

You should always design the results table before you start collecting measurements. Use the method for the investigation to help you to identify the variables and design the table.

Table 2.3 shows how to design a results table for the data.

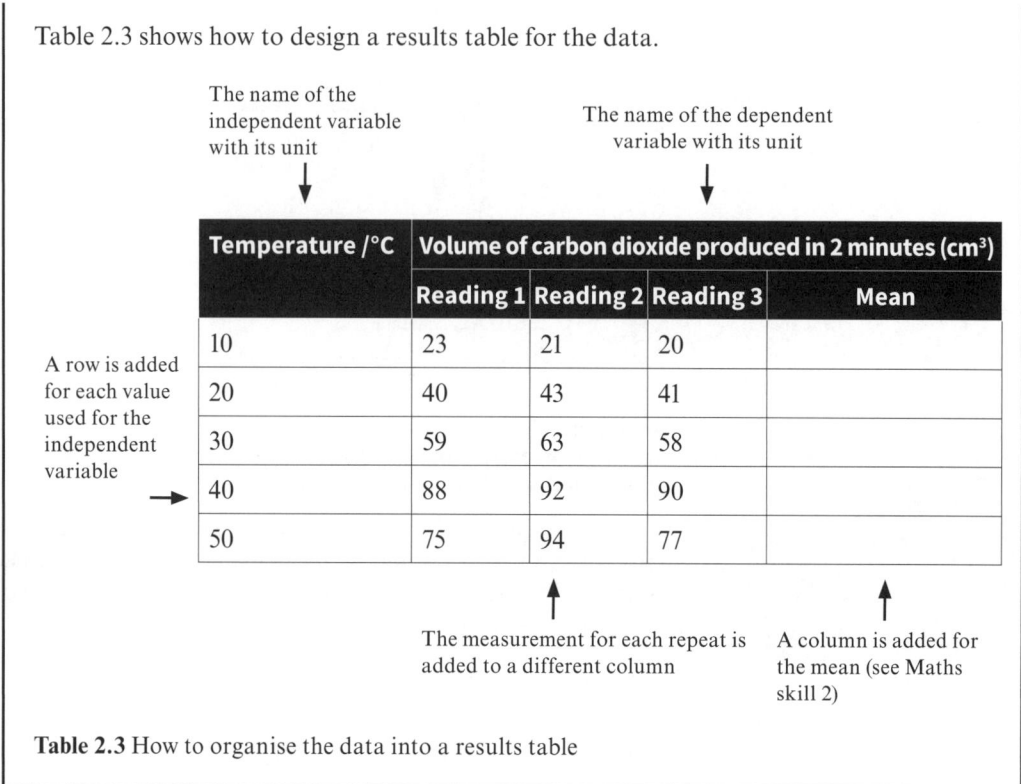

The name of the independent variable with its unit

The name of the dependent variable with its unit

A row is added for each value used for the independent variable

Temperature /°C	Volume of carbon dioxide produced in 2 minutes (cm³)			
	Reading 1	Reading 2	Reading 3	Mean
10	23	21	20	
20	40	43	41	
30	59	63	58	
40	88	92	90	
50	75	94	77	

The measurement for each repeat is added to a different column

A column is added for the mean (see Maths skill 2)

Table 2.3 How to organise the data into a results table

Practice question 12

Figure 2.16 shows the equipment some students used to investigate respiration.

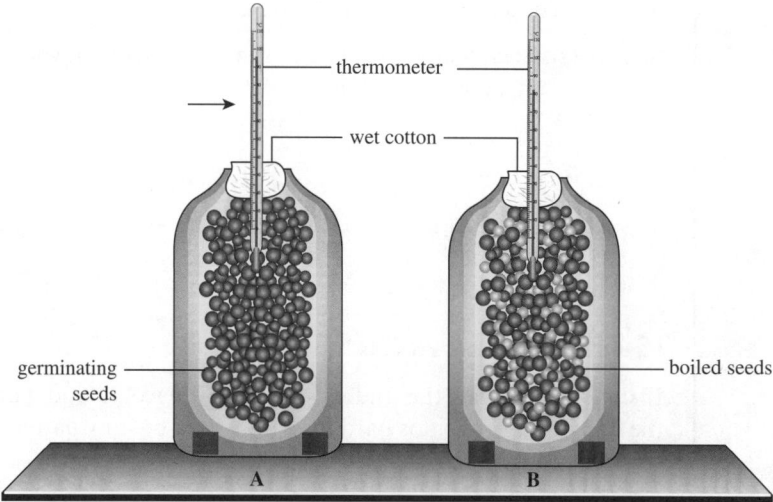

thermometer

wet cotton

germinating seeds

boiled seeds

A   B

Figure 2.16 Investigating respiration of seeds

The students displayed their results in the following table.

Type of seeds	Temperature		
	At start	At end	Rise
Germinating	21	45	
Boiled	22	22	0

a Identify the independent variable.

....

b Describe a mistake the students have made in designing the table.

....

c Calculate the temperature rise for the germinating seeds.

....

Practice question 13

A scientist investigated how the concentration of glucose affects aerobic respiration in yeast.

She measured the volume of oxygen used in cubic centimetres (cm^3) in 5 minutes.

She used glucose concentrations of $0.2\,g/cm^3$, $0.4\,g/cm^3$, $0.6\,g/cm^3$ and $0.8\,g/cm^3$.

She plans to take her measurements three times.

Design a table for her to record the results.

WATCH OUT

Make sure you use the term 'mean' and not 'average', because *average* has several different meanings.

Maths skill 2: Calculating the mean

TIP

Outliers are also known as **anomalous results.**

WORKED EXAMPLE 7

Let's return to the results table from the investigation in Worked example 6.

Temperature /°C	Volume of carbon dioxide produced in 2 minutes (cm^3)			
	Reading 1	Reading 2	Reading 3	Mean
10	23	21	20	
20	40	43	41	
30	59	63	58	
40	88	92	90	
50	75	94	77	

The next step is to calculate the mean volume of carbon dioxide produced at each temperature.

Here are the steps used to calculate the mean:

Step 1: Spot any outliers.

Outliers are results that are much larger or smaller than the other readings.

One of the readings for 50 °C is an outlier.

$94\,cm^3$ is much larger than both of the other readings. It is an outlier.

WATCH OUT

One reason why you should do a minimum of three readings is so you can spot outliers. If there are only two readings and there is a big difference between them, you would realise that one was an outlier but you would not be able to tell which one it was!

TIP

In step 3, do this calculation on your calculator. You will see that the number 3 is repeated many times. It is a *recurring* decimal. This is shown by the … at the end of the number.

32

TIP

Remember to round to an appropriate number of significant figures.

Step 2: Add together the readings.

For 10 °C the calculation would be:

$$23 + 21 + 20 = 64$$

Step 3: Divide the total by the number of repeats.

For 10 °C the calculation would be:

$$64 \div 3 = 21.333\ldots$$

Step 4: Use the correct number of significant figures in the answer.

The mean 21.333… needs to be **rounded** to the same number of significant figures as the measured result with the fewest number of significant figures. In this case all the results are to two significant figures.

So the mean would also be rounded to two significant figures, that is 21.

Practice question 14

Complete the means in the table:

Temperature /°C	Volume of carbon dioxide produced in 2 minutes (cm³)			
	Reading 1	Reading 2	Reading 3	Mean
10	23	21	20	21
20	40	43	41	
30	59	63	58	
40	88	92	90	
50	75	94	77	

Practice question 15

A student measured the mass of six grapes.

The masses were: 6.2 g, 5.4 g, 4.5 g, 4.9 g, 5.6 g, 6.3 g

Calculate the mean.

Further question

Hydrogen peroxide is produced during respiration. It is harmful, and must be removed.

Cells produce the enzyme catalase that catalyses the breakdown of hydrogen peroxide into water and oxygen.

A class investigated how the concentration of catalase affects the rate of breakdown of hydrogen peroxide. They used concentrations of 10 vol., 15 vol., 20 vol., 25 vol. and 30 vol. They measured the volume of oxygen produced after 30 seconds.

Figure 2.17 shows the equipment they used.

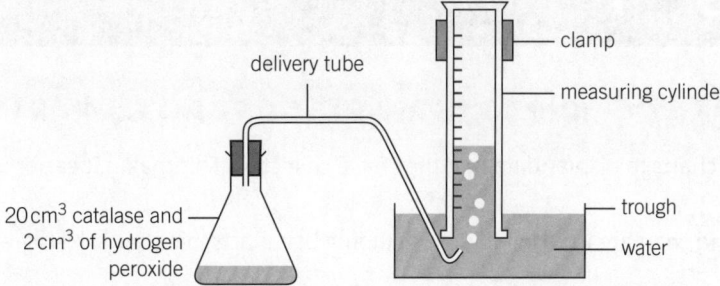

Figure 2.17 Apparatus for investigating how the concentration of catalase affects the rate of breakdown of hydrogen peroxide

a The class has a variety of measuring cylinders to choose from: $10\,cm^3$, $25\,cm^3$, $50\,cm^3$.

Write which measuring cylinder they should use to measure the volume of:

Catalase ....

Hydrogen peroxide ....

Oxygen produced in 30 seconds ....

b The class is asked to take their measurements three times.

In the following space, draw a suitable table to record their results.

c The results for 15 vol. of hydrogen peroxide from one student were:

$$12.6, 13.2, 7.2\,cm^3$$

Calculate the mean.

....

Why do you need to be able to draw graphs and charts in biology?

- Biologists use graphs and charts to display data that they have collected. This makes it easier to compare data and see patterns.
- Different types of graph and chart are used in biology, including bar charts, pie charts, histograms, line graphs and scatter graphs.
- The type of graph or chart chosen depends on the type of data.

Maths focus 1: Drawing bar charts

Bar charts

Bar charts are used to show data that can be sorted into different categories. This might be categorical or discrete data.

A bar chart can be used to compare the amount of fat in different foods; see Figure 3.1.

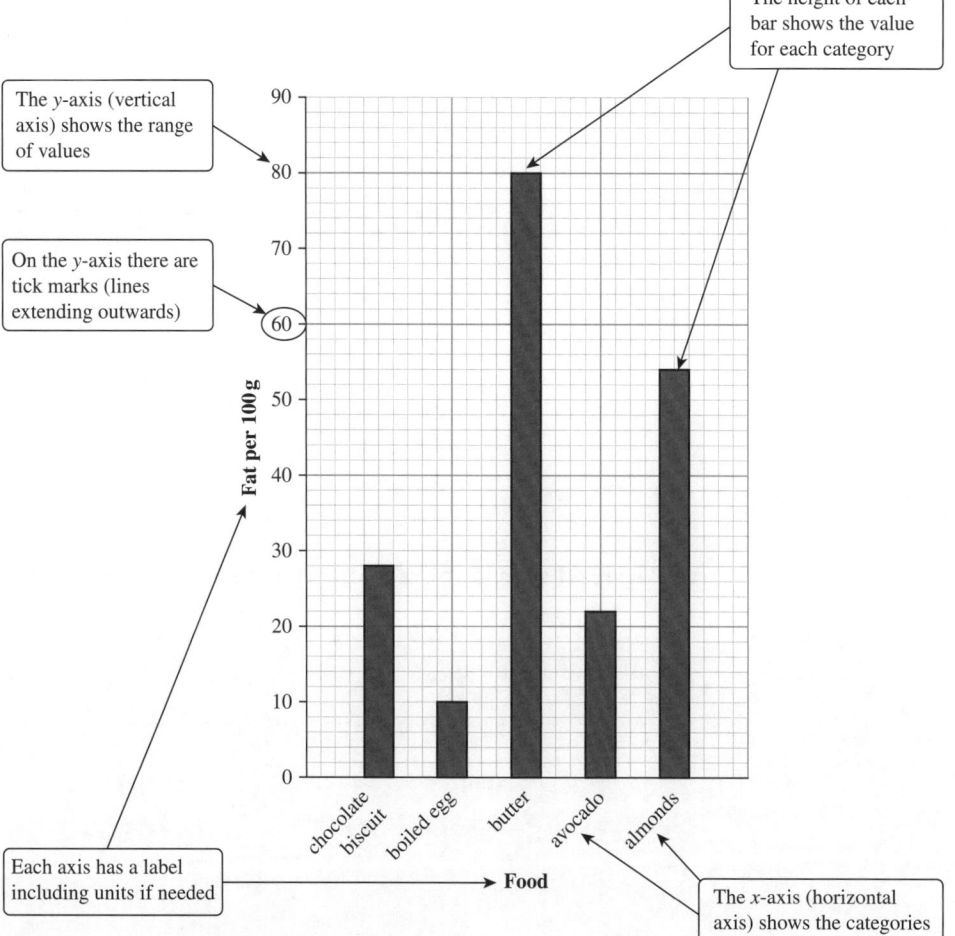

The y-axis (vertical axis) shows the range of values

On the y-axis there are tick marks (lines extending outwards)

The height of each bar shows the value for each category

Each axis has a label including units if needed

The x-axis (horizontal axis) shows the categories

Figure 3.1 A bar chart to show the amount of fat per 100 g of different foods

What maths skills do you need to draw a bar chart?

1	Choosing a suitable scale for the *y*-axis	• Choose the scale so all the data can be included
		• Aim to use as much of the graph paper as you can
		• Avoid scales that make the values hard to read
2	Drawing the bars	• Show each category by one bar
		• Make all the bars the same width and separate them with a gap
		• Draw the bars as accurately as you can to the correct height

Maths skill practice

How does drawing bar charts relate to discontinuous variation?

In biology you might collect data on variation in a group of people, animals or plants. Some of this data will be discontinuous, which means it can be sorted into categories. For example, a person's blood group is either A, B, AB or O. This is shown in Table 3.1.

Blood group	Number of people
A	24
B	6
AB	2
O	28

Table 3.1 Number of people with the different blood groups

Drawing a chart will show more clearly how many people have each blood group so you can compare them. The data are *categorical* so can be displayed using a bar chart.

Maths skill 1: Choosing a suitable scale for the *y*-axis

In the bar chart showing blood groups, the *y*-axis is going to display the *number of people*.

The lowest number of people is 2 and the highest is 28.

It is always best to start the *y*-axis at 0 (unless all the numbers are very large). So, for this bar chart the *y*-axis will start at 0 and go up to at least 28.

Graph paper is normally divided up into large squares; see Figure 3.2. Each square contains many smaller squares, normally: $10 \times 10 = 100$.

The side of each large square on the graph paper should have a value of 1, 2 or 5 multiplied by a power of 10.

TIP

The scale you choose depends on how big the numbers are that you need to show.

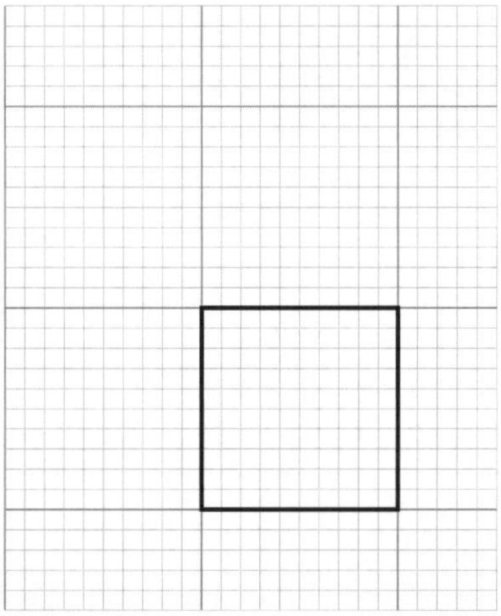

For example, you could choose:

	0.1	1	10	100, etc.
or	0.2	2	20	200, etc.
or	0.5	5	50	500, etc.

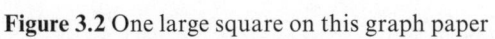

Figure 3.2 One large square on this graph paper

35

WORKED EXAMPLE 1

For the data on blood groups in Table 3.1, which of the scales shown in Figure 3.3 would you choose? Explain your choice.

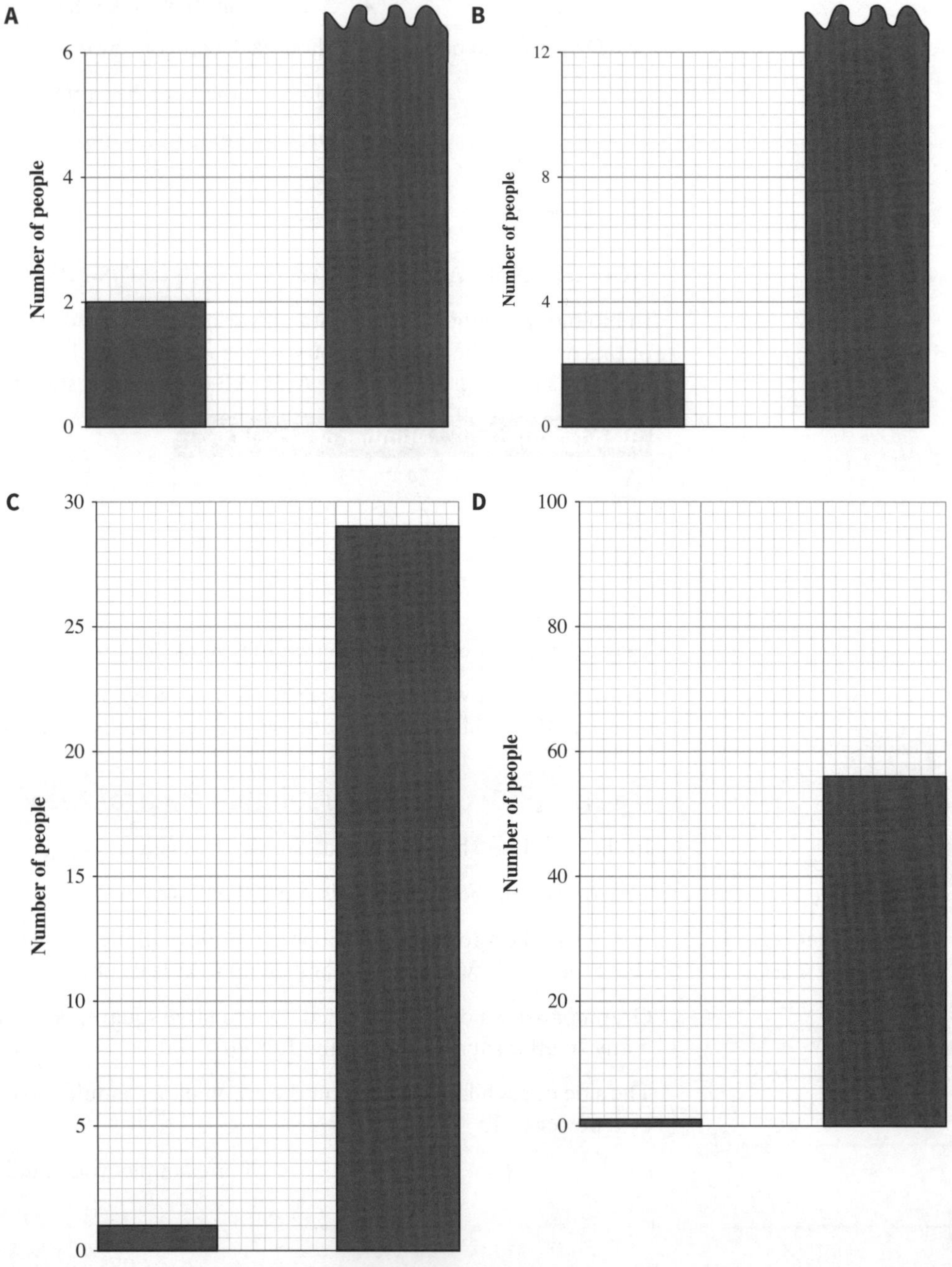

A

B

C

D

Figure 3.3 Different scales for drawing the y-axis

The scale in **C** would be the best choice.

This is because in A and B the scales mean that the bar for 28 people will not fit on the paper.

The scale in D means that the bar for two people is too small to read easily.

TIP

The **axis** with the scale you have chosen should take up over half of the space you have been given, whether this is a whole sheet of graph paper or the graph paper drawn on an exam paper.

WATCH OUT

Make sure you leave enough space to write the title of the y-axis next to it.

Practice question 1

Some people can roll their tongue and others cannot.

The number of students who can or can't roll their tongue in a class was counted.

The data are shown in Table 3.2.

Tongue roller	Number of students
yes	18
no	12

Table 3.2 Results for a survey on tongue rolling

Which y-axis scale (**A–C**) is the best choice to display this data?

Draw a circle around the correct letter.

A

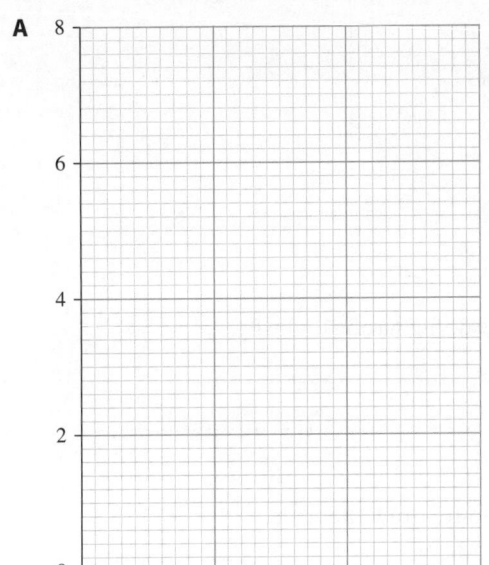

B

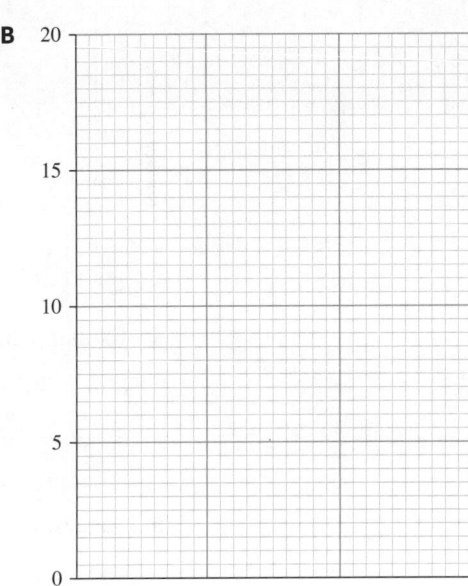

C

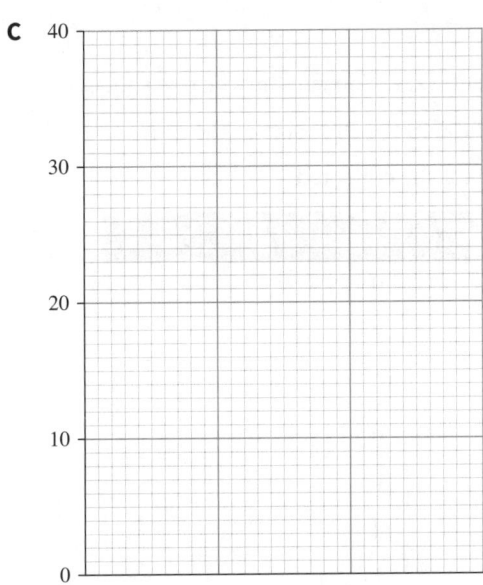

Practice question 2

A student collected data on the colour of flowers on different pea plants.

His data are shown Table 3.3.

Colour of flowers	Number of plants
white	82
yellow	26
red	14

Table 3.3 Results for a survey on the colour of flowers

He starts to write the scale on the *y*-axis on the graph paper as shown below.

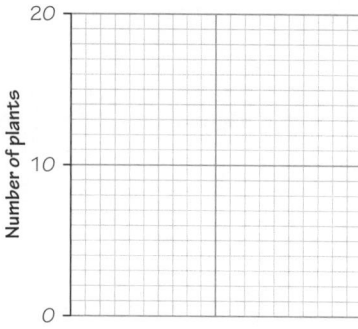

a Explain what he is doing wrong and why.

....

....

....

b Suggest how he should draw the scale.

....

Practice question 3

Shoes come in different sizes. You can only be one shoe size.

A student collected data on the shoe size of the girls in her class.

Table 3.4 shows the data she collected.

Shoe size	Number of girls
35	0
36	3
37	10
38	6
39	6
40	4
41	1
42	0

Table 3.4 Results for a survey on shoe size

TIP

The *y*-axis is drawn vertically using a ruler.

On the following graph paper, draw a suitable *y*-axis which can be used to show the data as a bar chart.

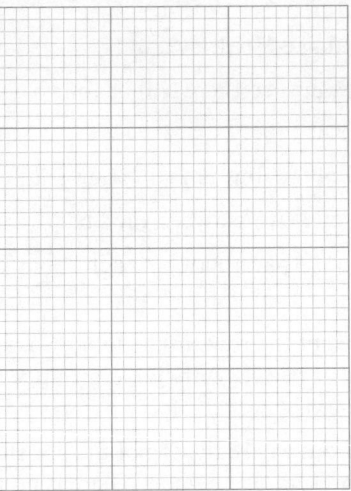

Maths skill 2: Drawing the bars

Draw bars to extend from the *x*-axis.

Each bar represents one category.

The height of the bar shows the value for each category.

WORKED EXAMPLE 2

39

If we return to the blood group data from Table 3.1, we can see the steps needed to draw the bars.

Blood group	Number of people
A	24
B	6
AB	2
O	28

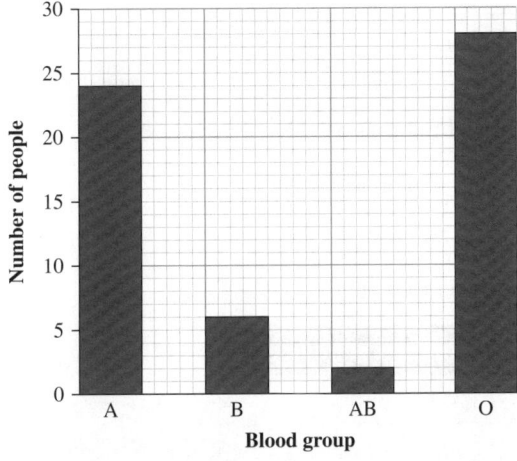

Figure 3.4 A bar chart to show the number of people with different blood groups

Step 1: Draw a line for the *x*-axis.

TIP

Make sure all the bars will fit onto the graph paper.

The bars all need to be the same width.

KEY QUESTIONS TO ASK YOURSELF:

1   How many bars will you need to draw?

   There are four blood groups, so there will be four bars.

2   How wide will each bar be?

   Work out how you will fit the four bars on your grid.

3   How much space will you leave between each bar?

   Allow the same amount of space between each.

Step 2: Draw the bars in order of the rows in the table. So, for this chart the first bar will show the number of people with blood group A. Use a ruler to draw the first bar next to the y-axis.

Use the scale to work out where the top of the bar should be. Using this scale, two *small* squares represent one person. There is no need to colour the bars in.

Step 3: Underneath the bar, write the name of the category.

Step 4: Leave a gap and draw the next bar. The size of the gap is not important, as long as the bars are not touching.

Step 5: Underneath the x-axis, write the label (copy this from the table). For this chart, it is 'Blood group'.

TIP

The categories can also be numbers. This is called *discrete* data.

Practice question 4

A student collected data on the number of boys in each year in his school.

His data are shown in the table.

Year	Number of boys
7	120
8	89
9	101
10	117
11	95

He draws a bar chart.

a   State the title of the x-axis. ....

b   State the name of the first bar he will draw. ....

Practice question 5

The student then collected data on how many boys in the school were left or right handed.

His data are shown in the table.

Handedness	Number of boys
Right	354
Left	168

Complete the bar chart to show the data.

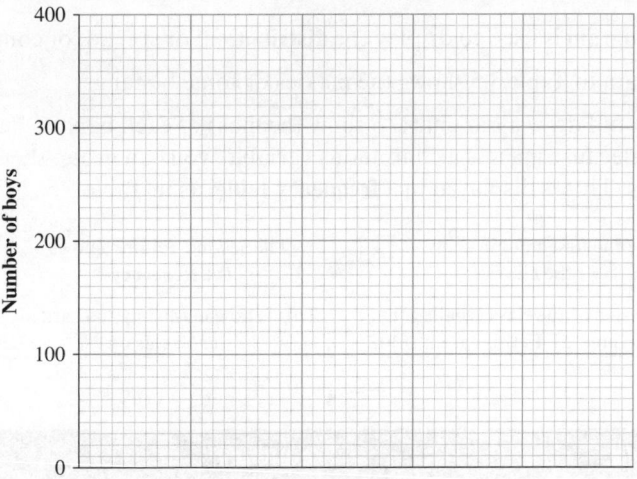

Practice question 6

The student collected data on how many brothers or sisters (siblings) the students in his class had.

His data are shown in the table.

Number of siblings	Number of students
0	2
1	12
2	11
3	4
4+	1

Draw a bar chart to show the data.

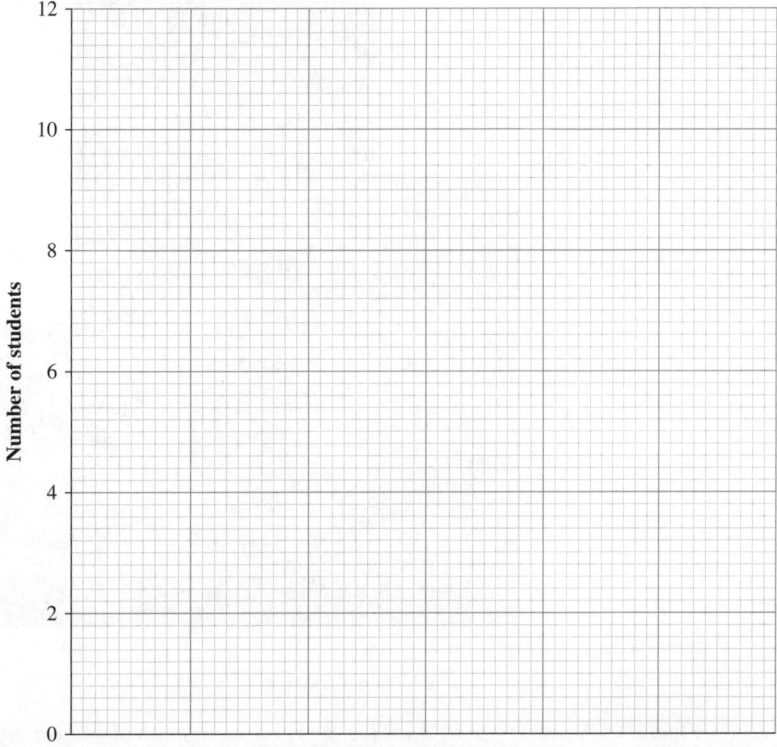

Maths focus 2: Drawing histograms

A **histogram** is used to display the **distribution**, or spread, of continuous data.

The data in Table 3.5 shows the masses of some bananas.

You could draw a bar chart to show the mass of each banana but that would contain a lot of bars. Because mass is a continuous variable, you can group them together into groups called **classes**. This is displayed in a **frequency table**, as in Table 3.5.

The first column shows the *classes*.

The size of the class is called the class interval. In this case it is 10.

The second column shows the **frequency**.

This is how many bananas are in each class.

Mass/g	Frequency
110–119	3
120–129	6
130–139	5
140–149	2

Table 3.5 Frequency table of masses of bananas

These data can be used to draw a histogram, which shows the spread of the data as in Figure 3.5.

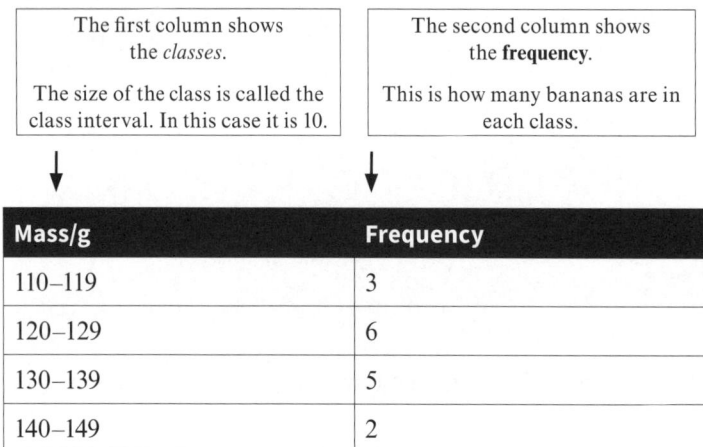

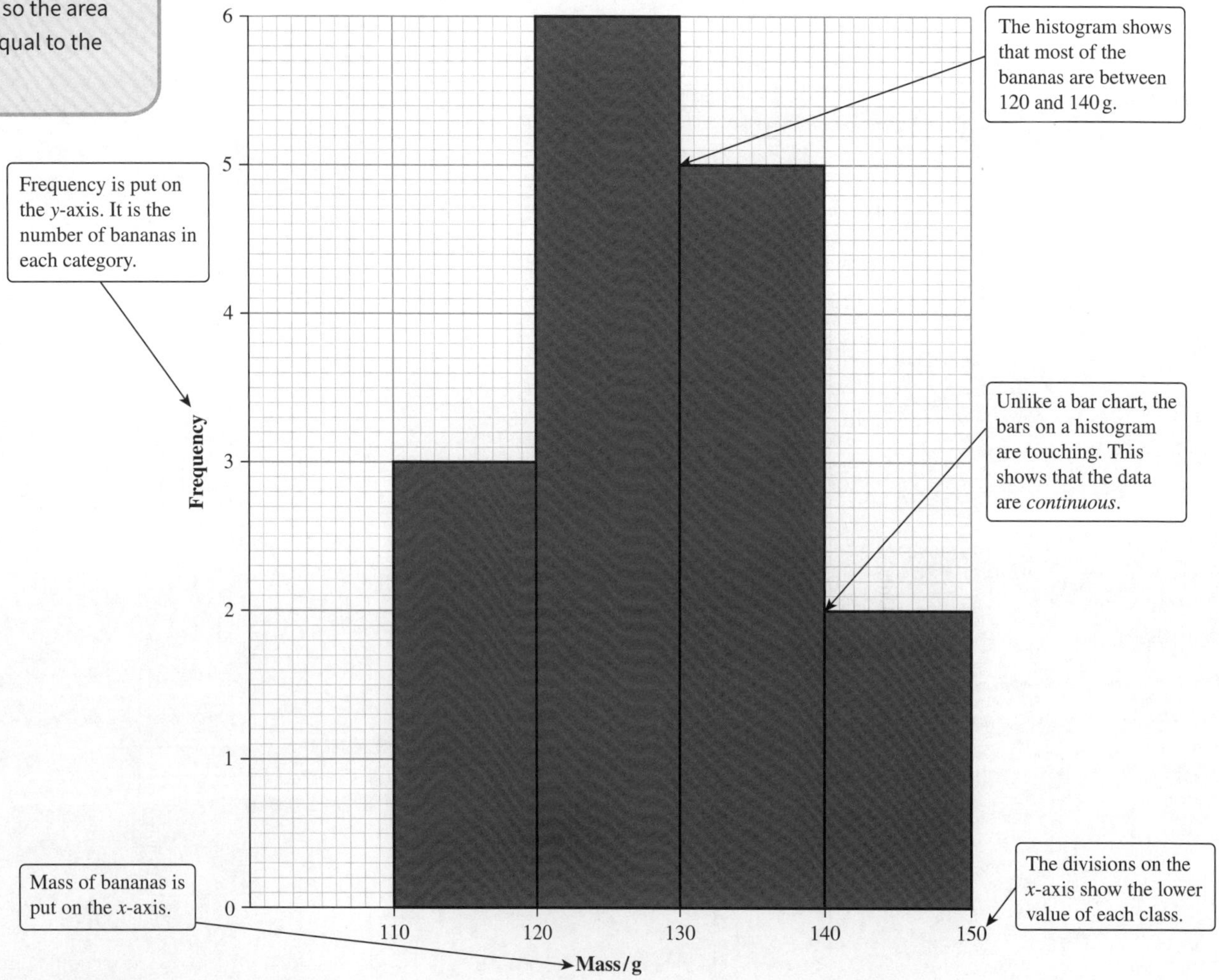

The histogram shows that most of the bananas are between 120 and 140 g.

Frequency is put on the *y*-axis. It is the number of bananas in each category.

Unlike a bar chart, the bars on a histogram are touching. This shows that the data are *continuous*.

Mass of bananas is put on the *x*-axis.

The divisions on the *x*-axis show the lower value of each class.

Figure 3.5 A histogram to show the distribution in mass of some bananas

WATCH OUT

There are differences between the meaning of 'histogram' in mathematics and science. In mathematics the widths of each column are different from each other, because their *area is equal to the value*. In science the bars are the same height, so the area is *not* equal to the value.

What maths skills do you need to draw a histogram?

1 Putting the data into classes	• Choose the class interval so there are neither too few nor too many classes
	• The frequency of each class is worked out
2 Drawing the histogram	• The classes are put on the x-axis
	• The bars are drawn to show the frequency of each class
	• The bars must be touching

Maths skill practice

How does drawing histograms relate to continuous variation?

When you study variation, some of the data you collect will be continuous. Examples include the height of plants, the hand span of people or the mass of fruit.

Maths skill 1: Putting the data into classes

WORKED EXAMPLE 3

The data below shows the height of a group of 15–16 year olds.

Height/cm	154, 156, 164, 151, 142, 168, 165, 170, 156, 151, 145, 142, 158, 171, 149, 165, 169, 157

Drawing a histogram will show more clearly the distribution of height in the class. This will show if more people are shorter or taller, and the most common height. This pattern can then be compared to another class, or even the whole country.

Step 1: Write the data out in order:

Height/cm	142, 142, 145, 149, 151, 151, 154, 156, 156, 157, 158, 164, 165, 165, 168, 169, 170, 171

Step 2: Now you can choose your class intervals. You should choose a size that gives you not too few or too many classes. A total of 4–6 classes is a good number.

Height/cm	142, 142, 145, 149,	151, 151, 154, 156, 156, 157, 158,	164, 165, 165, 168, 169,	170, 171
Classes	140–149 cm	150–159 cm	160–169 cm	170–179 cm
Freq.	4	7	5	2

Step 3: Finally, you can work out the frequency in each class. This is how many heights fall into each class. For example, there are 4 in the 140–149 cm class.

Practice question 7

The data show the length of the middle finger of a group of women.

Length of middle finger/cm	7.7	6.8	6.5	7.9	8.1	7.5	7.2	6.6	7.8	6.4	7.9	8.0	7.5	7.9	8.2

Complete this frequency table.

Length of middle finger/cm	Frequency
6.0–6.4	
6.5–6.9	
7.0–7.4	
7.5–7.9	
8.0–8.5	

Practice question 8

The data show the mass of a collection of tortoises living in a zoo.

The zoo keeper wants to display the data as a histogram.

Mass of tortoise/g	125	101	123	130	142	100	155	158	154	146	132	129

a The zoo keeper starts to draw a frequency table.

Complete the classes in the first column.

Mass of tortoise/g	Frequency
100–114	

b Suggest why the zoo keeper chose this class interval.

....

Practice question 9

A student measured the length of the leaves on a bamboo shoot.

The table shows her data, in order of length.

Length of leaf/mm	50	51	53	57	59	63	63	64	66	68	70	71	72	72	73	73

Choose suitable class intervals and draw a frequency table to display the data.

Maths skill 2: Drawing the histogram

WORKED EXAMPLE 4

Let's return to the data we looked at in Maths skill 1, Worked example 3, about the height of a group of 15–16 year olds.

Here is the frequency table for the data.

Height/cm	Frequency
140–149	4
150–159	7
160–169	5
170–179	2

Step 1: Draw the *y*-axis.

Frequency is plotted on the *y*-axis, so look at the highest and lowest frequency in the table.

In this example, the highest frequency is 7. Each large square has the value of 1.

Make sure you label the y-axis 'Frequency'.

Step 2: Draw the *x*-axis.

The divisions on the *x*-axis show the class intervals.

The first number will be the smallest value of your first class.

In this example it is 140 cm. You do not have to start this axis at 0.

The lowest value of the next class is 150, so this is the value you write in the next large square. Each large square in this histogram has the value of 10.

Label the *x*-axis with the variable and unit.

Step 3: Draw the bars.

The height of each bar represents the frequency of that class, see Figure 3.6.

Unlike a bar chart, the bars need to be touching.

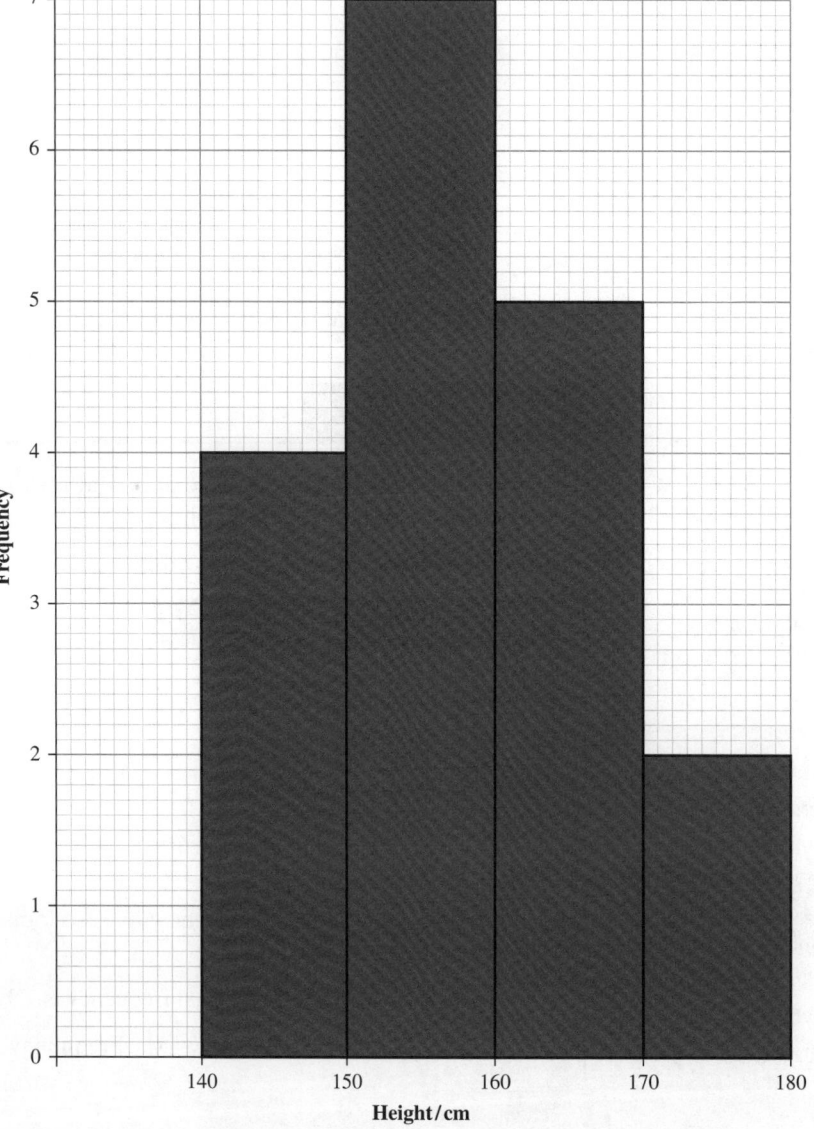

Figure 3.6 A completed histogram to show the heights of a class of students

WATCH OUT
The data in the table uses decimal numbers, but the method used is exactly the same as with whole numbers.

Practice question 10

A student collected data on the students in her class.

She started with hand span. The data she collected is shown in the frequency table.

Hand span/cm	Frequency
15.0–16.9	2
17.0–18.9	5
19.0–20.9	8
21.0–22.9	5
23.0–24.9	3

Complete the histogram on the axes below.

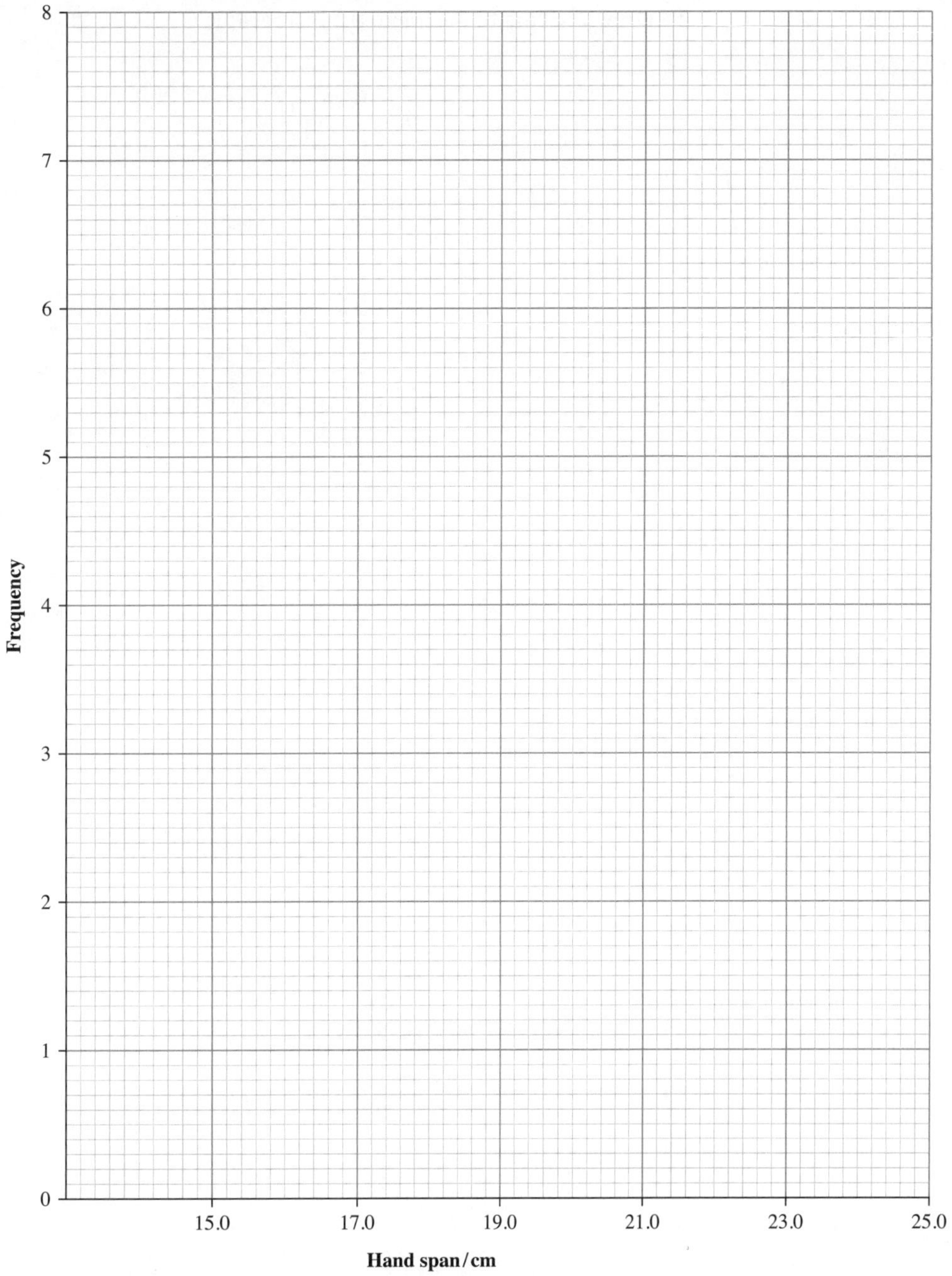

Practice question 11

The student then measured the length of the students' right feet.

The data she collected is shown in the frequency table.

Foot length/mm	Frequency
200–219	1
220–229	4
230–239	12
240–249	6
250–259	1

a On the graph below, draw the scale and title for the *x*-axis.

b Draw the bars to complete the histogram.

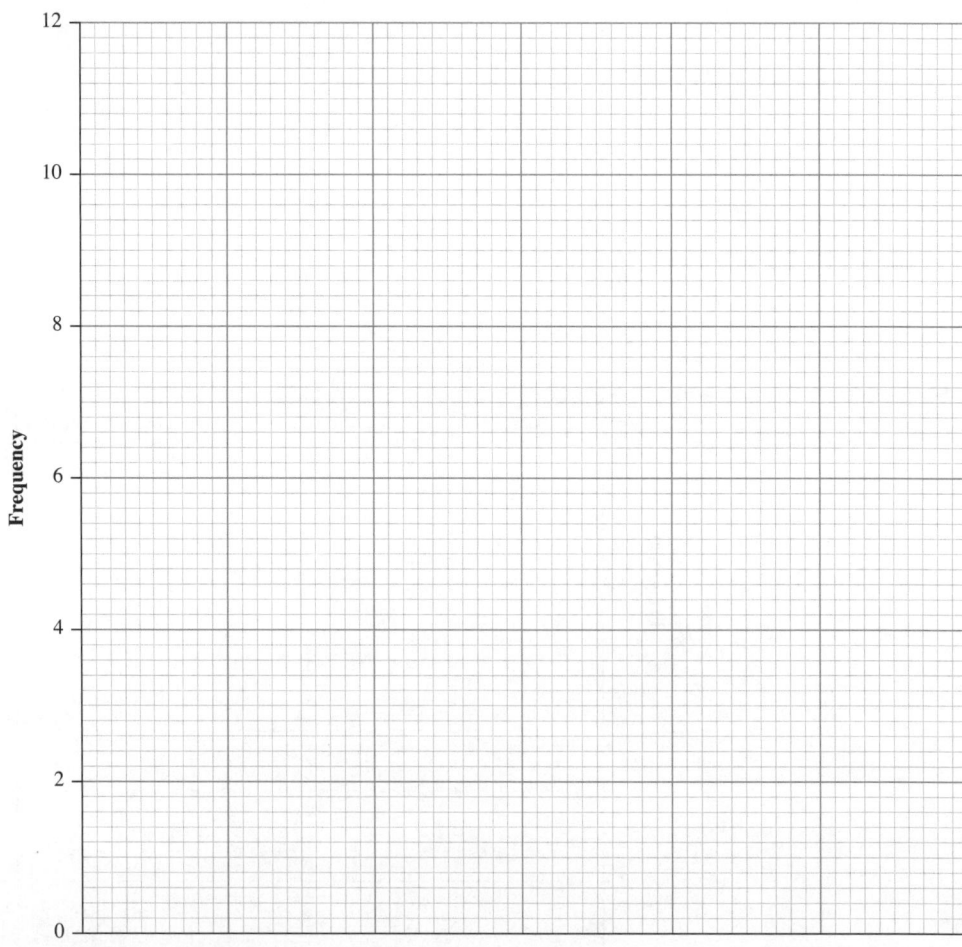

Practice question 12

Finally, she measured the resting heart rate of the students in her class.

The data are shown in the table.

Resting heart rate/beats per minute	Frequency
50–59	1
60–69	9
70–79	8
80–89	9
90–99	4
100–109	3

Draw a histogram to show the data on the graph paper below.

LINK

See Chapter 2,
Maths focus 3
'Recording and
processing data' for
more information.

Maths focus 3: Drawing line graphs

Line graphs are very common in biology. They are used to show the relationship between two continuous variables: the independent and the dependent variable.

For example, a line graph can be used to show how the mass of a fetus changes over the weeks it is in the womb (see Figure 3.7).

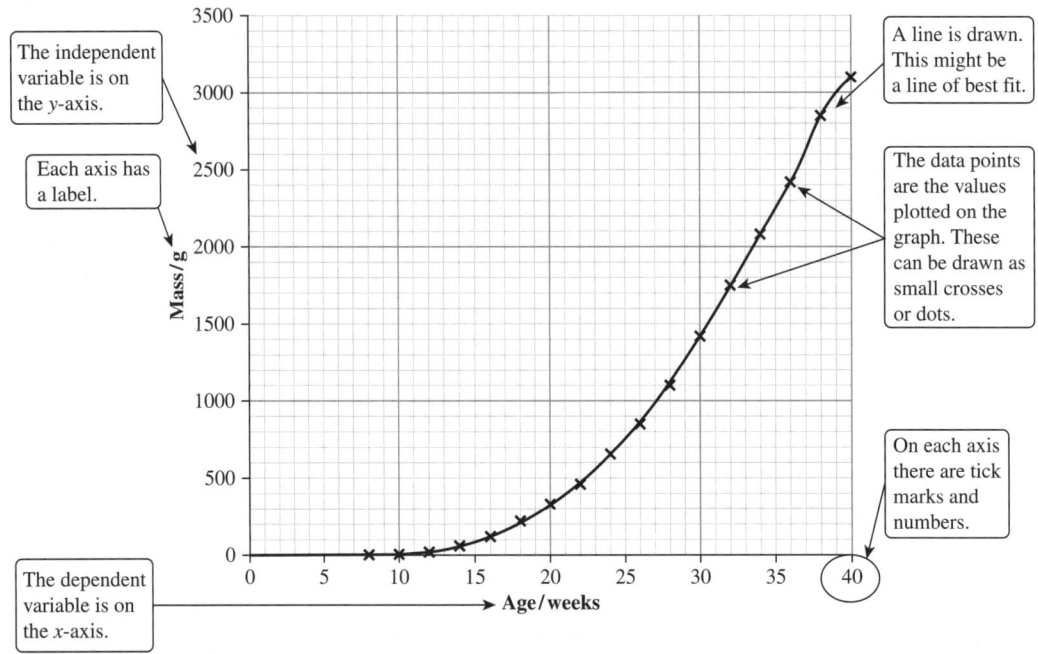

Figure 3.7 A graph to show the change in mass of a fetus

This line graph shows how the mass (in grams) of a fetus changes with its age (in weeks).

The mass of the fetus is the dependent variable. The age of the fetus is the independent variable.

Graphs in biology can show how something varies over time. Here, time is the independent variable and so is plotted on the *x*-axis.

What maths skills do you need to draw a line graph?

1	Drawing the axes	• Decide which variable goes on which axis
		• Choose the range of each axis
		• Choose an appropriate scale
2	Plotting the data points	• Accurately plot each data point
3	Drawing the line or curve of best fit	• Know how to draw a line or curve of best fit

LINK

More about interpreting line graphs is covered in Chapter 4, 'Interpreting data'

LINK

See Maths focus 1, Maths skill 1, 'Choosing a suitable scale for the *y*-axis', to remind yourself about this.

Maths skill practice

How does drawing line graphs relate to photosynthesis?

When you study photosynthesis you will carry out many investigations and gather data.

You will investigate how different variables, such as light intensity and temperature, affect the **rate** of photosynthesis (i.e. how quickly it takes place).

Using the data to draw line graphs will help you to work out relationships between the variables and also calculate how they affect the rate of photosynthesis.

Maths skill 1: Drawing the axes

WORKED EXAMPLE 5

A student investigated the relationship between light intensity and volume of oxygen produced by the pondweed *Elodea* during photosynthesis.

Figure 3.8 shows the equipment he used.

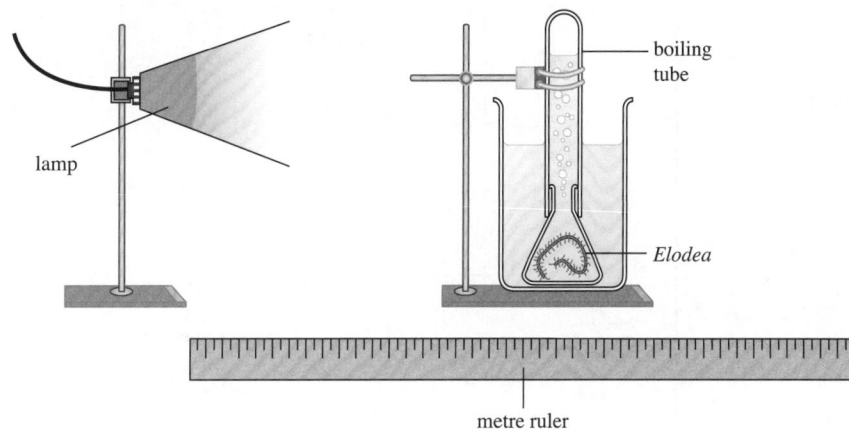

Figure 3.8 The equipment used to investigate how light intensity affects the rate of photosynthesis

Table 3.6 shows the results.

Distance between lamp and plant/cm	Number of bubbles produced in 1 minute
10	56
20	28
30	24
60	18
80	10
100	6

Table 3.6 Results from an investigation into how light intensity affects the rate of photosynthesis

Draw the axes for a graph of this data.

TIP

You should start each axis at the **origin** (0, 0).

TIP

Don't forget to label the axes including units. You can use the headings from the table.

51

WATCH OUT

In Table 3.6, the values for the dependent variable do not increase by equal amounts: 10, 20, 30, 60, 80, 100. You must *not* plot these values on the x-axis, but instead make sure each large square has the same value, such as 0, 20, 40, 60, 80, 100.

Sometimes the independent variable in a table might not be in numerical order. For example, the student may have chosen to use a distance of 100 cm, not 10 cm first. Even if this is the case, you must always draw the axes so they start at 0 and then increase as you go along.

WATCH OUT

For some graphs an axis might contain negative numbers. Figure 3.9 shows an example.

Step 1: First, you need to decide which is the dependent variable and which is the independent variable.

In this example, the lamp's distance from the plant was the variable being changed by the students so this is the *independent* variable. It goes on the x-axis.

The number of bubbles produced in 1 minute changed as a result of moving the lamp, so this was the *dependent* variable. This goes on the y-axis.

Step 2: Next, you will need to work out a suitable scale for each axis. This is the same skill you learnt about previously when drawing bar charts. The only difference is, with a line graph, you will also need to choose a scale for the x-axis.

Figure 3.9 shows axes suitable for plotting a line graph of this data.

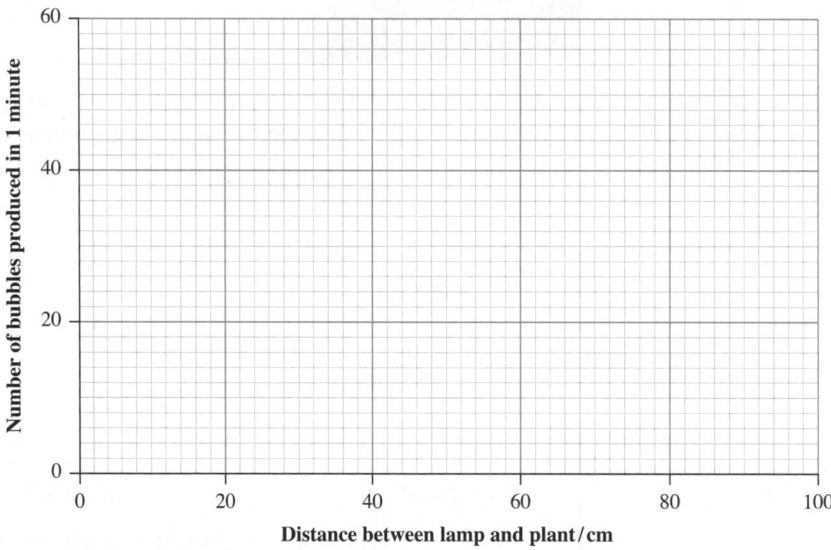

Figure 3.9 The x and y-axes for an investigation into how light intensity affects the rate of photosynthesis

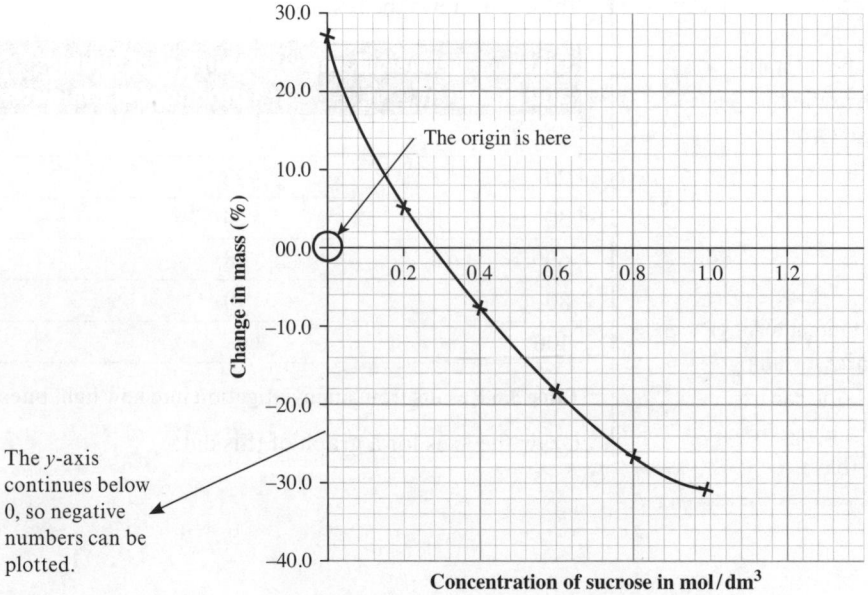

Figure 3.10 Change in mass of potato at different sucrose concentrations

Practice question 13

A student investigated how the amount of carbon dioxide affected the rate of photosynthesis.

He changed the concentration in the water surrounding a piece of *Elodea* and kept the light intensity the same. He measured the volume of oxygen produced in 1 minute.

a What independent variable did he use? Circle the letter of your choice.

A Light intensity

B Length of the *Elodea*

C Volume of oxygen produced in 1 minute

D Concentration of carbon dioxide

b After collecting his results, he decided to draw a line graph.

State what variable he should plot on the:

i *y*-axis ....

ii *x*-axis ....

Practice question 14

The light intensity (in lux) of a point in a forest was measured over a period of 24 hours.

The following sketch shows the axis labels for a line graph of the results.

Describe the mistake made in the labels.

....

....

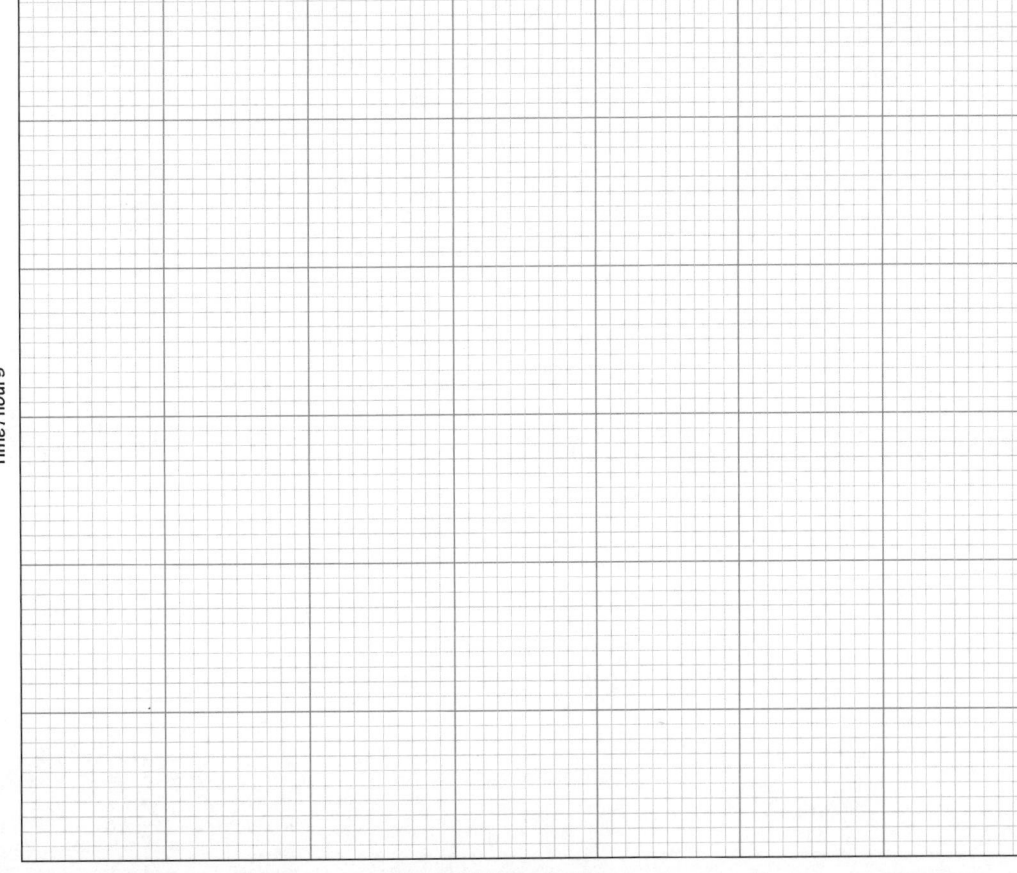

Light intensity / lux

Practice question 15

A student investigates the effect of temperature on the rate of photosynthesis.

The table shows his results.

Temperature/°C	Number of oxygen bubbles produced in 1 minute
10	16
20	25
30	33
40	43
50	0

Complete the axes below. You should:

• Decide which variable to plot on which axis.

• Choose a suitable scale for both axes and write numbers and tick marks on them.

• Write labels for each axis.

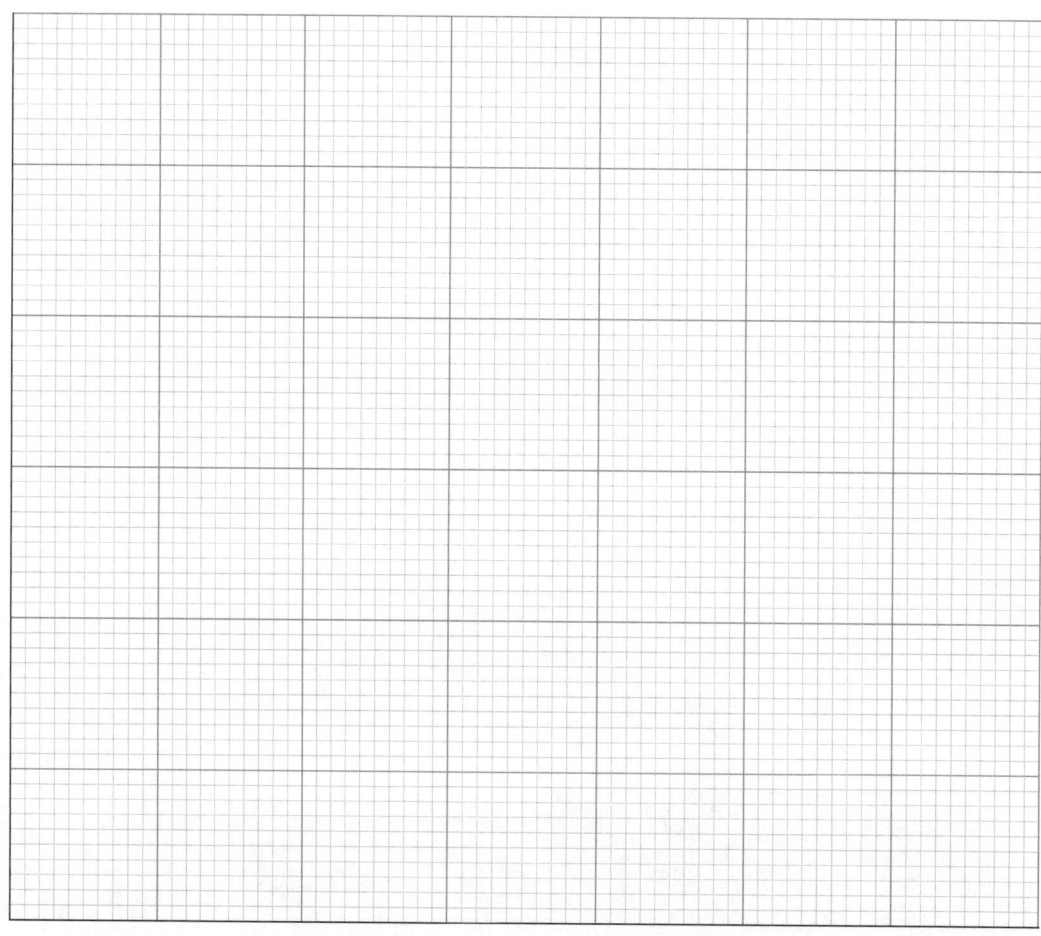

Maths skill 2: Plotting the data points

WORKED EXAMPLE 6

Return to the data in Worked example 5; the first data point is in the first row of the table and is (10, 56). See Figure 3.11.

Figure 3.11 How to plot data points

To plot this data point, find where 10 is on the *x*-axis and then travel up this line until you reach 56 on the *y*-axis. Draw a cross or a small dot with a circle drawn around it so the middle of the cross or dot is where these lines meet.

Continue until you have plotted all the data points.

Use a ruler to guide you along the lines if you find it difficult.

Practice question 16

A student found the following results table on the internet.

Carbon dioxide concentration/%	Rate of photosynthesis/units
0	0
0.02	20
0.04	34
0.06	40
0.08	45
0.1	48
0.12	50

She plotted the data on a line graph.

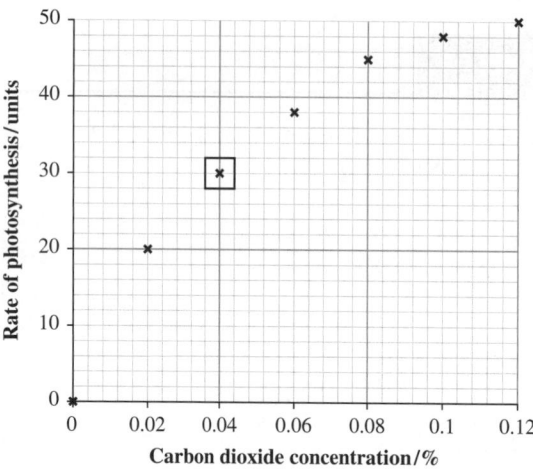

Circle any data points she has plotted incorrectly.

Practice question 17

A student plotted his results from an investigation on photosynthesis.

His graph is shown below.

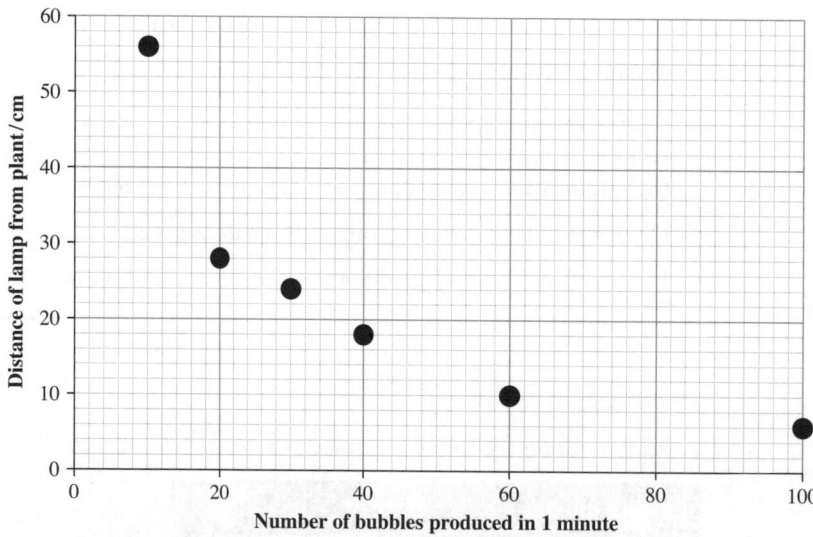

a Describe what he has done wrong.

....

b Explain what he should do to correct his mistake and why it is important he does.

....

....

....

....

Practice question 18

The table shows some results for an investigation on photosynthesis.

Light intensity/units	Number of oxygen bubbles produced per minute
1	2
3	12
5	24
8	38
10	45
12	45

Complete the following graph by drawing the remaining data points, using information from the table above.

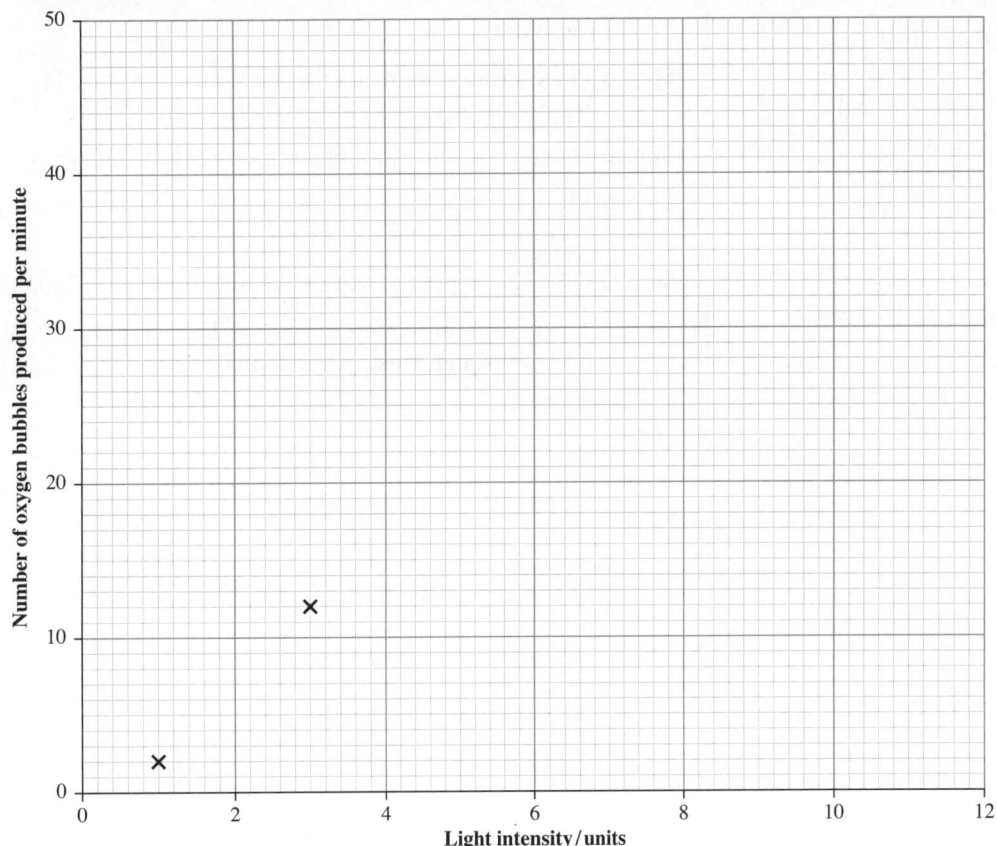

Maths skill 3: Drawing the line or curve of best fit

1 Joining the points

In biology the data you collect might be taken at intervals over time. For example, pollution levels once a month, or population size once every 5 years.

The data points should be joined with straight lines. The line could be straight (see Figure 3.12a), curved (see Figure 3.12b) or go up and down in a zig-zag (see Figure 3.12c).

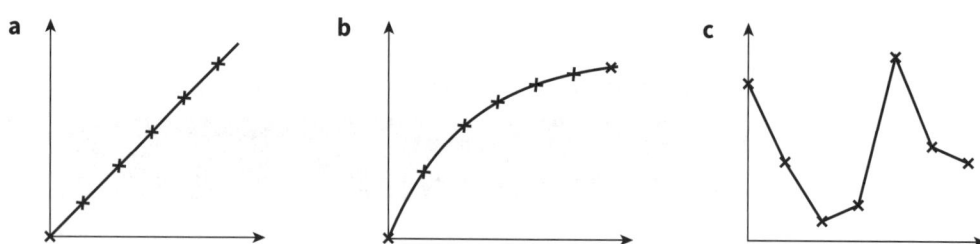

Figure 3.12 Graph **a** is a straight-line graph, graph **b** is curved, graph **c** goes up and down

2   **Drawing a best-fit line**

Most of the line graphs you draw in biology are using results from an investigation where one variable affects another. In this case the data points will not be accurate because of errors, so you will draw a **best-fit line** to show the trend of the data.

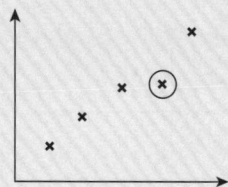
WORKED EXAMPLE 7

Follow these steps:

Step 1: Place a transparent ruler along the data points. This will allow you to see all the points so you can judge where to draw the line.

Step 2: Decide if the line should go through the origin (0, 0).

Step 3: Move the ruler so there are roughly the same number of points, evenly spread, above and below the line.

Step 4: Use a sharp pencil to draw the line, see Figure 3.13.

The best-fit line could be a curve. The same rules apply – try to draw a line that passes through most of the points.

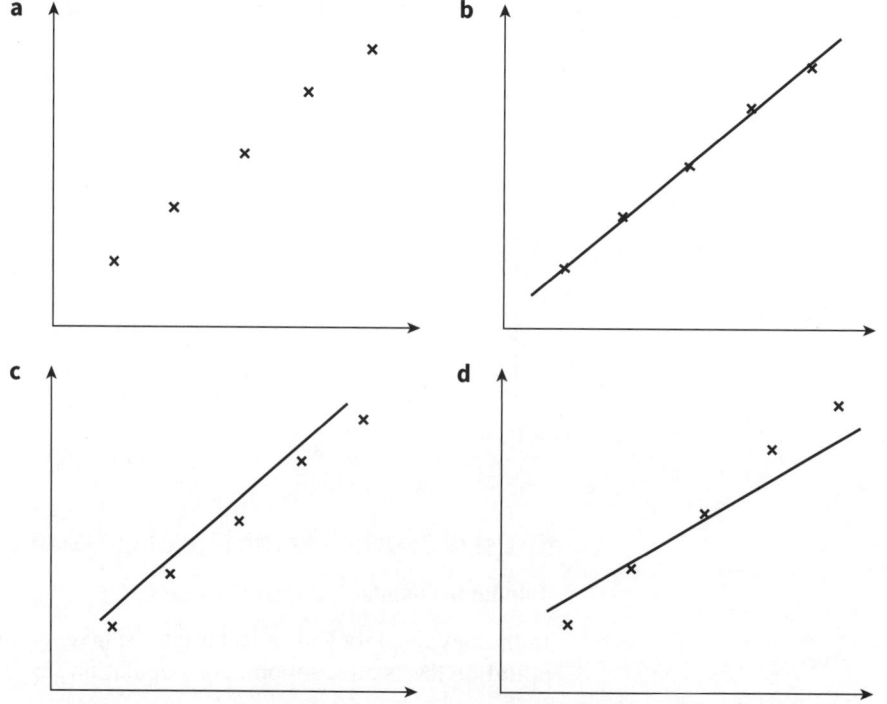

Figure 3.13 The line drawn in **b** is an example of a good best-fit line. **c** and **d** are not good best-fit lines in **c** the line is too high and in **d** the line has the wrong gradient (steepness)

Practice question 19

A student plotted the results from a photosynthesis investigation.

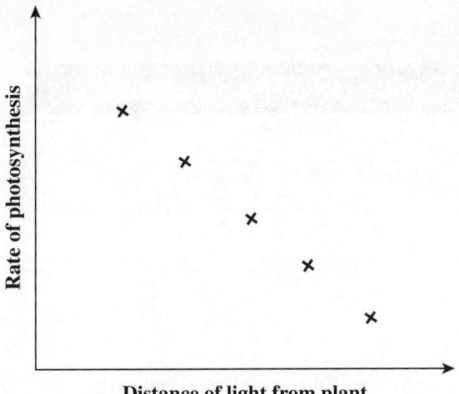

Draw a best-fit line on the graph.

Practice question 20

The graph below shows the results from an investigation into how temperature affects the rate of photosynthesis.

Draw a curve of best fit on the graph.

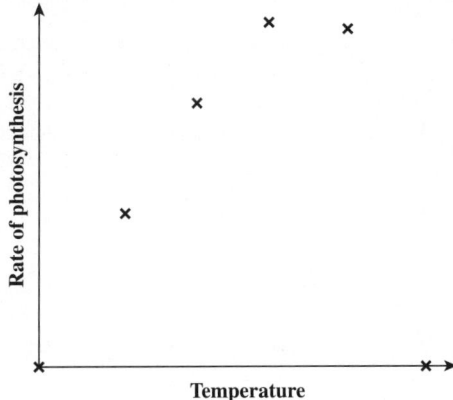

Practice question 21

Draw a curve of best fit on the graph.

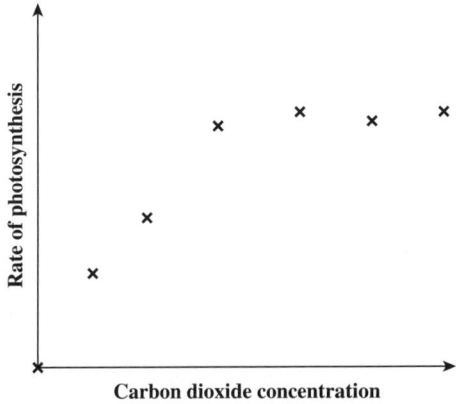

Further question

The pulse rate of a person was measured as they took part in some different activities.

The table shows the results.

Activity	Pulse rate/beats per minute
sitting	67
walking slowly	75
running	98
climbing stairs	89

On the graph paper below draw a bar chart of the results.

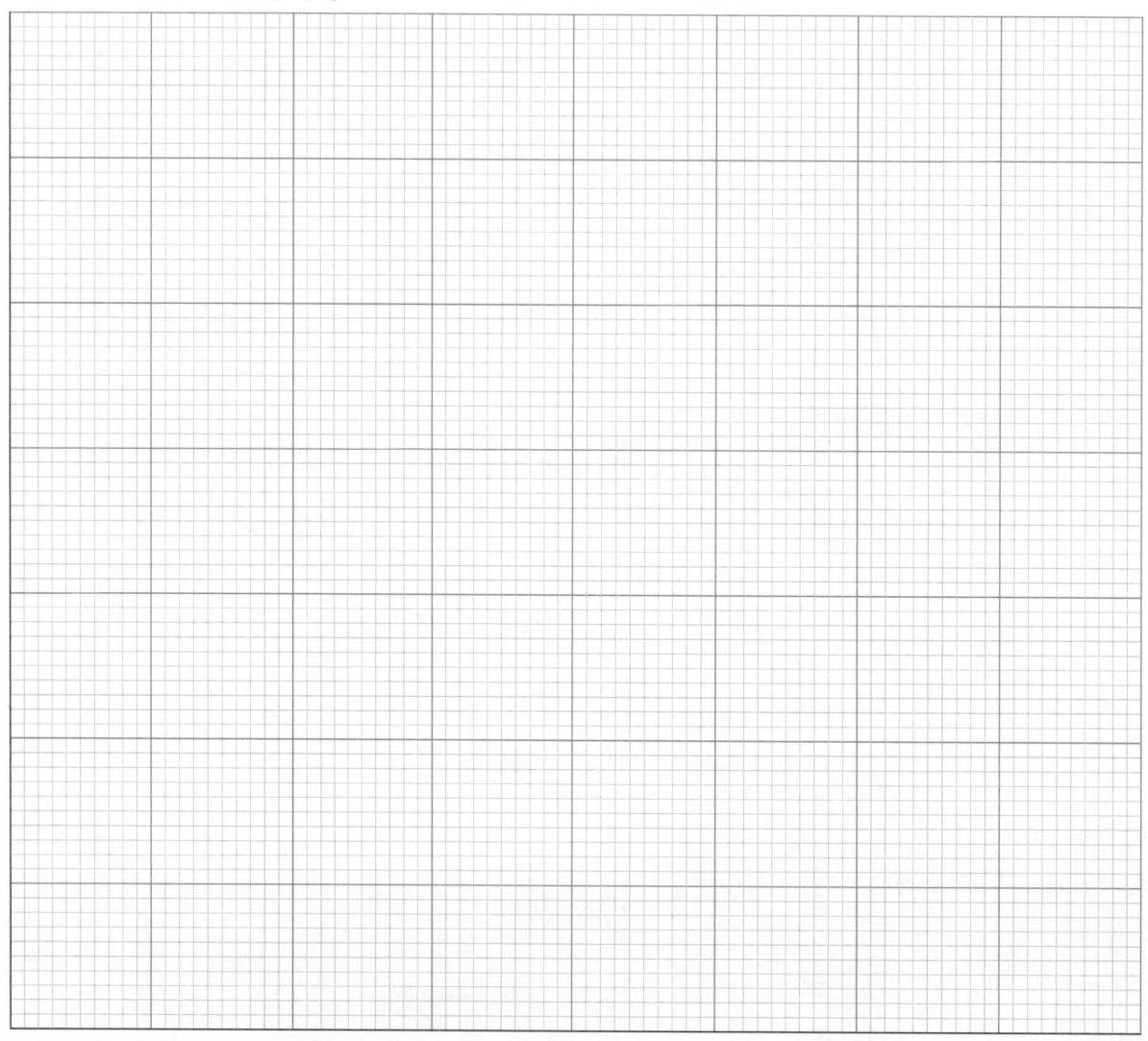

Chapter 4:
Interpreting data

Why do you need to interpret data in biology?

- Biologists collect data and display it as graphs and charts.
- The next step in an investigation is to interpret what the data shows.

Maths focus 1: Interpreting bar charts, histograms and pie charts

LINK

The types of data are covered in detail in Chapter 2, Maths focus 1, 'Naming types of data'.

Bar charts and pie charts are used to display *categorical* data.

Histograms look like bar charts, but they show the distribution of *continuous* data.

What maths skills do you need to interpret bar charts, histograms and pie charts?

LINK

How to draw bar charts and histograms is covered in Chapter 3, 'Drawing graphs and charts'.

1	Identify the categories	•	Read the titles of the *x*-axis (for bar charts and histograms)
		•	Read the key if there is one
2	Describe what the data shows	•	Compare the height of the bars/sizes of the segments
		•	Use the *y*-axis on bar charts and histograms to read values

Maths skills practice

How does looking for patterns in bar charts, histograms and pie charts relate to human health?

61

Maths skills 1 and 2: Identify the categories and describe what the data show

WORKED EXAMPLE 1

Figure 4.1 shows a bar chart – how do you interpret the data?

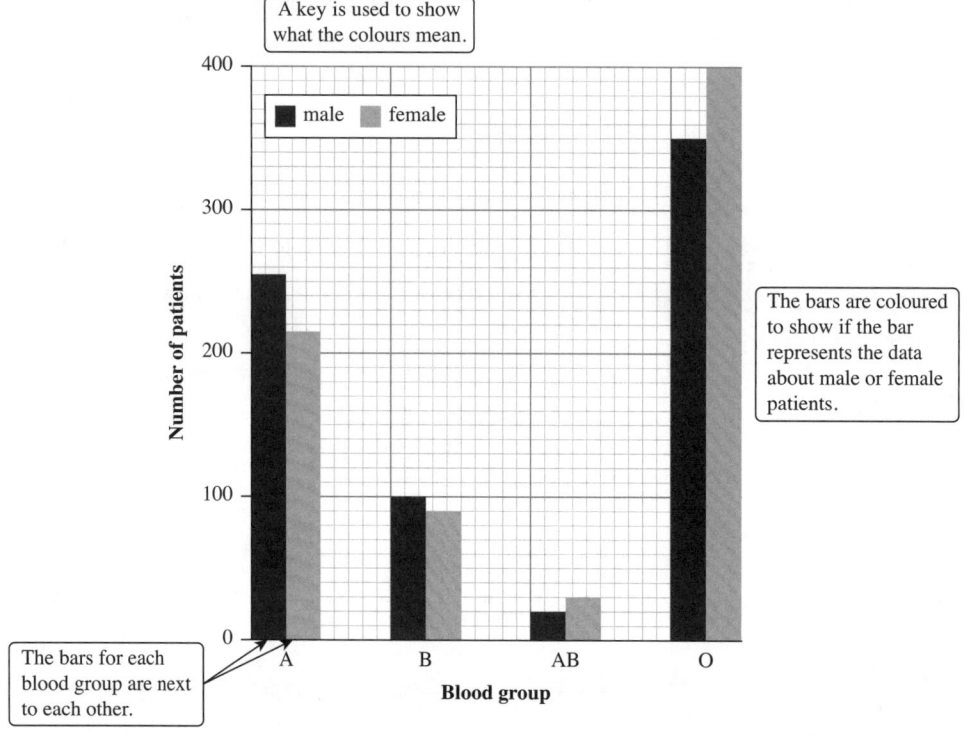

A key is used to show what the colours mean.

The bars are coloured to show if the bar represents the data about male or female patients.

The bars for each blood group are next to each other.

Figure 4.1 A bar chart to show the number of male and female patients with different blood groups

These are the steps you should take to interpret the data:

Step 1: Identify the categories.

Look at the title of the *x*-axis and the key (if there is one).

This bar chart has two categories. The *x*-axis shows one: blood group.

The key shows the other: the gender of the patient.

Step 2: Describe what the data shows.

Comparing the heights of the bars tells you some information.

For example, blood group O is the most common and AB is the least common.

Using the *y*-axis to read values allows you to discuss the data quantitatively (with numbers).

For example, for blood group A: 250 patients are male and 215 are female.

TIP

In a histogram, the height of the bars shows the frequency of values in each class.

TIP

If the sections in a pie chart are representing percentages, then they must add up to 100%. You can use this information to calculate any missing percentages.

WORKED EXAMPLE 2

Figure 4.2 is a **pie chart** that shows the causes of premature death by illness in the UK.

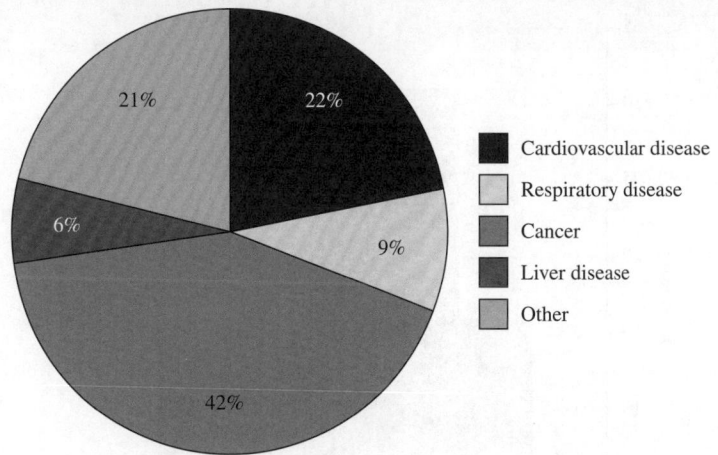

Cardiovascular disease
Respiratory disease
Cancer
Liver disease
Other

Figure 4.2 Causes of premature deaths by illness in the UK

How do you interpret the data?

These are the steps you should take:

Step 1: Identify the categories.

Each segment in the pie chart is one illness that causes premature death.

Step 2: Describe what the data shows.

Comparing the size of the segments shows you some information.

For example, cancer causes the most deaths. Liver disease causes the fewest.

Using the percentages allows you to discuss the data quantitatively (with numbers).

For example, cancer (42%) causes twice as many deaths as other causes (21%).

WATCH OUT

Be careful when describing what pie charts show. For example, you cannot say that cancer causes the most premature deaths. It causes 42%, but the other causes add up to 58%.

63

Practice question 1

A website contains the following pie chart, which shows the amounts of foods needed for a healthy diet.

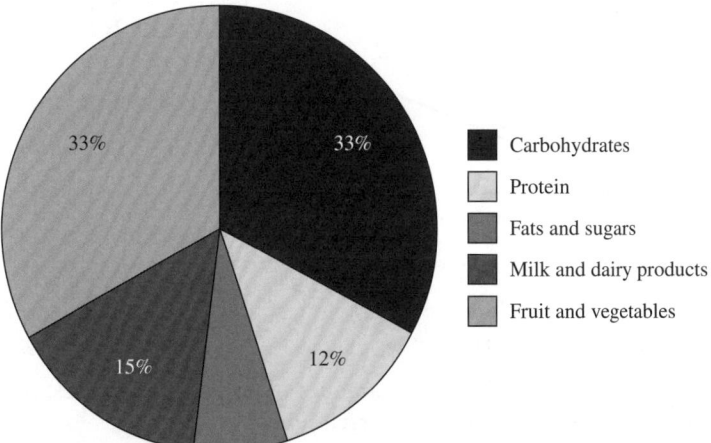

Carbohydrates
Protein
Fats and sugars
Milk and dairy products
Fruit and vegetables

Calculate the percentage of fats and sugars.

Practice question 2

100 adult men from the USA had their body mass index (BMI) measured.

The histogram shows the results.

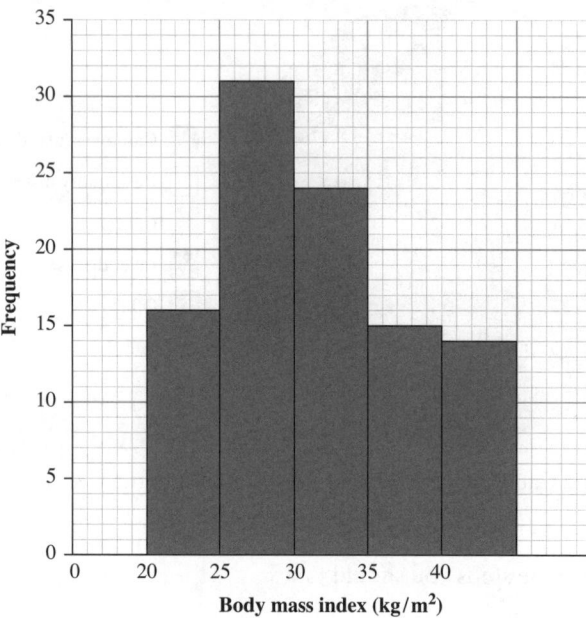

How many men had a body mass index of:

a more than $40\,\text{kg/m}^2$? ....

b between 20 and $30\,\text{kg/m}^2$? ....

Maths focus 2: Interpreting relationships in graphs

Line graphs are used to show how variables are related.

The shape of the graph shows the relationship, also called **correlation**.

The shape may show a **positive relationship** as in Figure 4.3a, or a **negative relationship** as in Figure 4.3b.

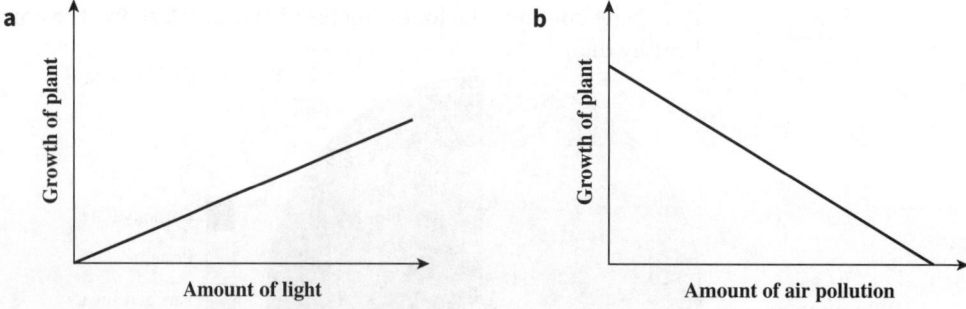

Figure 4.3 Line graphs show the relationships between variables

Graph 4.3a shows that as the amount of light increases, the growth of the plant increases. This is a *positive* correlation.

Graph 4.3b shows that as the amount of pollution increases, the growth of the plant decreases. This is a *negative* correlation.

What maths skills do you need to interpret relationships shown in graphs?

1	Interpreting straight-line graphs	• Name the variables
		• Identify the correlation shown in the graph
		• Describe what the correlation shows you about how the variables are related
2	Interpreting more complex line graphs	• Split the line into sections, so each section has a different trend
		• Consider gradients and rates of change
		• Tell the 'story' of the graph
3	Interpreting **scatter graphs**	• Is there a correlation between the data points?
		• How strong is it?
		• What does the correlation show?

Maths skill practice

Line and scatter graphs show the relationship between two variables. You can use the line to work out values not represented in the original data. This is called **interpolation** and **extrapolation**. The shape of the line shows how the variables are related.

How does looking for relationships in data relate to transport in animals?

Heart rate can be affected by many different variables, including exercise. These relationships can be identified by studying line graphs.

Coronary heart disease is a very common illness. Biologists study different variables to see if there is a link between the variable and an increased risk of a person developing the illness.

Maths skill 1: Interpreting straight-line graphs

WORKED EXAMPLE 3

A student carried out an investigation using water fleas.

She changed the temperature of the water around the flea and measured its heart rate by using a microscope to view the heart and count the number of beats per minute.

Figure 4.4 shows her results.

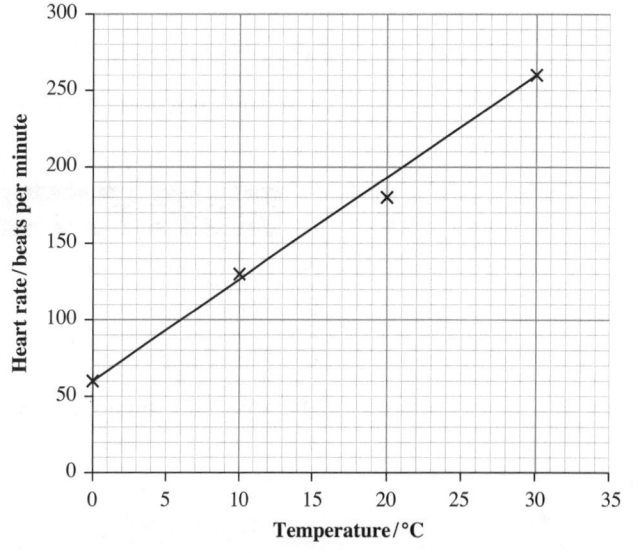

Figure 4.4 A line graph to show how temperature affects the heart rate of a water flea

> **TIP**
>
> In biology, line graphs often have best-fit lines. You can use the best-fit line to identify the correlation.

TIP

If the graph is a straight line going through the origin (0, 0), then you can say the relationship is **directly proportional** (see Figure 4.5). This means that as one variable is doubled (or multiplied by n), the other variable doubles (or is multiplied by n).

The **ratio** (change in y)/(change in x) is always the same, here it is $\frac{2}{10} = 0.2$. This is the value of the **gradient**.

KEY QUESTIONS TO ASK YOURSELF:

- What are the variables?
- What correlation is shown by the graph?
- What does this correlation show you about how the variables are related?

The independent variable is temperature; this is what was changed.

The dependent variable is heart rate; this is what was measured.

The line shows a positive correlation.

So, as the temperature increased, the heart rate increased.

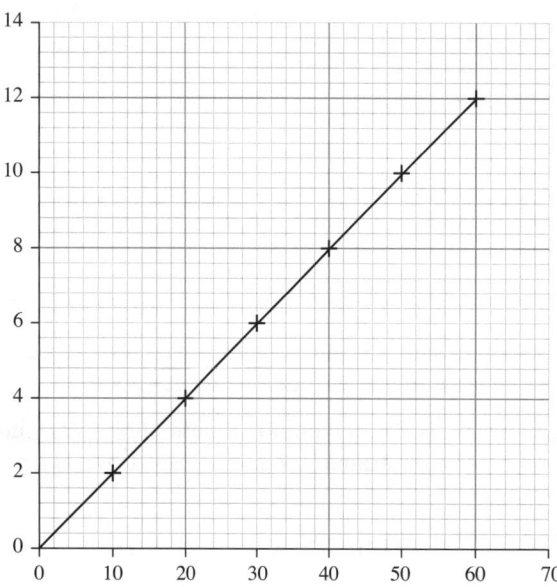

Figure 4.5 A line graph showing a directly proportional relationship. As the value on the x-axis increases by a value of 10, the value on the y-axis increases by a value of 2.

Practice question 3

A student investigated how the concentration of ethanol affected the heart rate of a flea.

What row in the table correctly identifies the variables he used? Circle the correct letter.

	Independent variable	Dependent variable
A	Temperature of ethanol	Heart rate
B	Heart rate	Concentration of ethanol
C	Heart rate	Temperature of ethanol
D	Concentration of ethanol	Heart rate

Practice question 4

The graph shows the student's results from the investigation in the previous question.

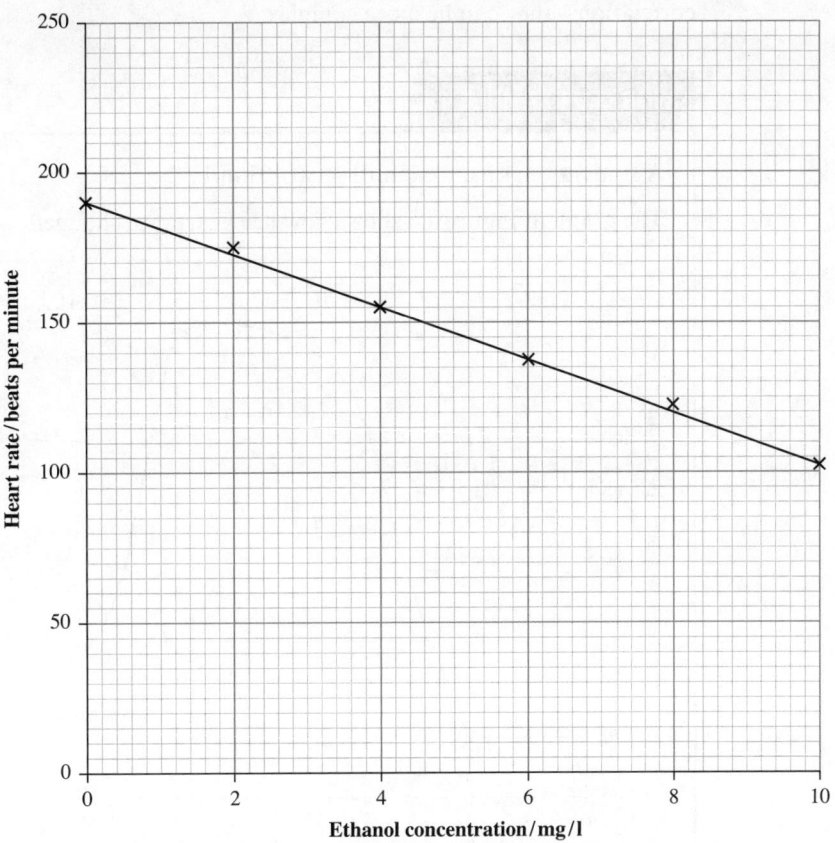

What type of correlation is shown by the graph?

....

Practice question 5

Use the graph to explain the relationship between the variables.

....

Maths skill 2: Interpreting more complex line graphs

Many of the line graphs you use in biology are not straight lines showing a simple correlation – they can be more complex.

WORKED EXAMPLE 4

A student ran on a treadmill set at 10 km/h.

The graph in Figure 4.6 shows how her heart rate changed.

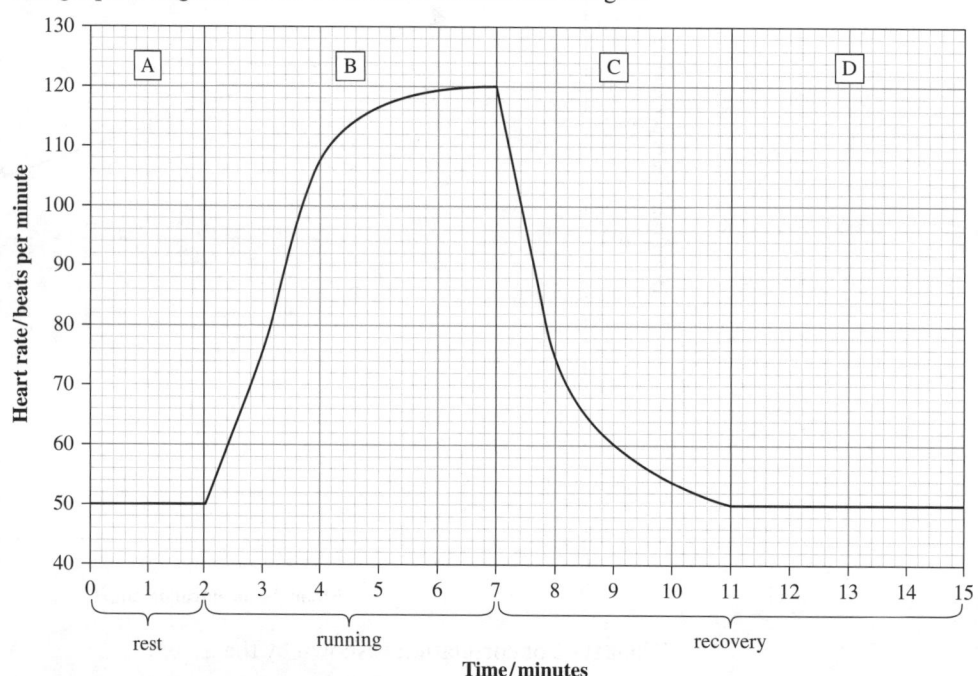

Figure 4.6 A line graph to show how the heart rate of a student on a treadmill changes

KEY QUESTIONS TO ASK YOURSELF:

- Can the line be split up into sections?
- Does the x-axis have a unit of time? If so, does the steepness, known as the gradient, of the line change?
- What is the 'story' of the graph?

This graph has four different sections. The line in each section shows a different trend. By describing the trend in each section, you can tell the 'story' of the graph.

Section A: Between 0 and 2 minutes the heart rate stays at 50 beats per minute.

Section B: Between 2 and 7 minutes the heart rate increases to 120 beats per minute.

Between 2 and 4 minutes the line has a steep gradient. This shows that the heart rate is increasing at a fast rate.

Between 4 and 7 minutes the gradient is less steep. This shows that the heart rate is increasing at a slower rate.

Section C: Between 7 and 11 minutes the heart rate decreases back to 50 beats per minute.

- Can you describe how the gradient changes and what this shows?

Section D: Between 11 and 15 minutes the heart rate stays at 50 beats per minute.

WATCH OUT

You only need to consider gradient if the unit on the x-axis is a unit of time. This is because the gradient shows how the *rate* changes.

TIP

In some questions, you might be asked to explain the pattern in the graph. For this graph, you would be asked to explain why heart rate increases while exercising.

68

Practice question 6

Caffeine is a drug found in cola.

A student measured his heart at rest for 5 minutes and then drank some cola. He continued to measure his heart rate at regular intervals.

His results are shown below.

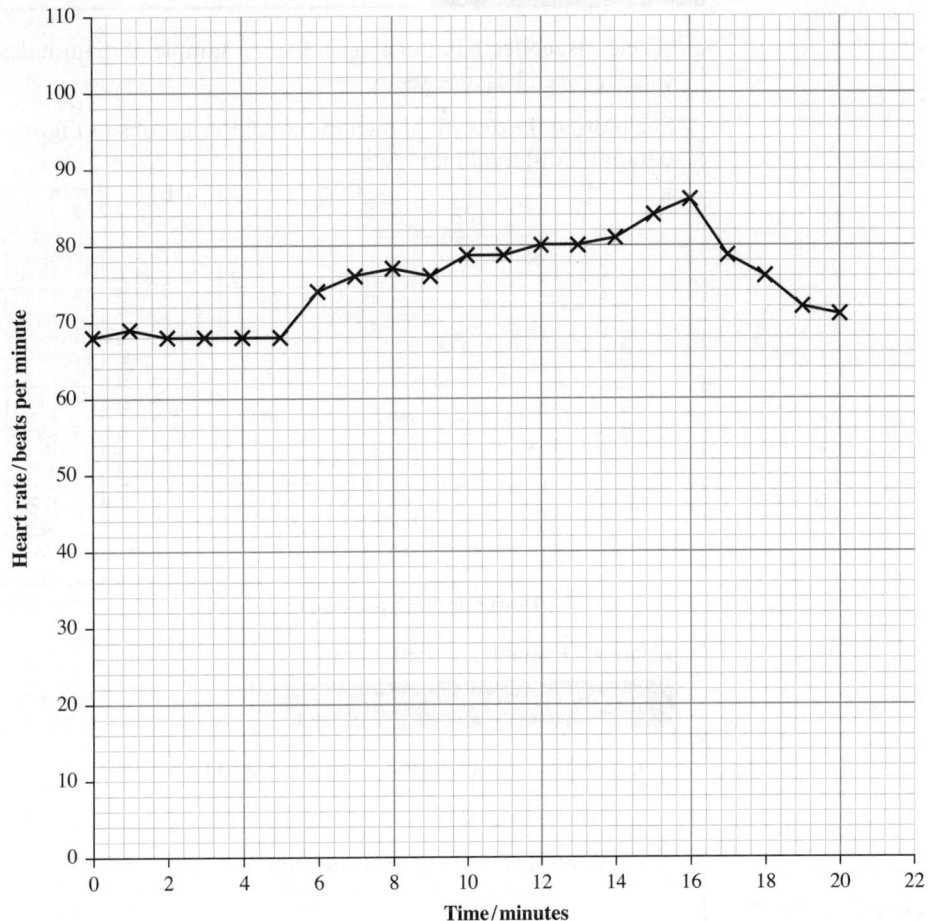

What happened to his heart rate between 0 and 5 minutes? Circle the correct letter.

a It increased.

b It decreased.

c It stayed constant.

d It decreased then increased.

Practice question 7

Explain how the graph in the previous question provides evidence that caffeine increases heart rate.

....

....

Maths skill 3: Interpreting scatter graphs

Scatter graphs are useful for looking at the relationship between two variables from the same sample of individuals.

WORKED EXAMPLE 5

A scientist collected information from a sample of mammals: lifespan, heart rate and time between heart beats.

She plotted the data as shown in the scatter graphs in Figure 4.7. Each cross shows the data for a different mammal.

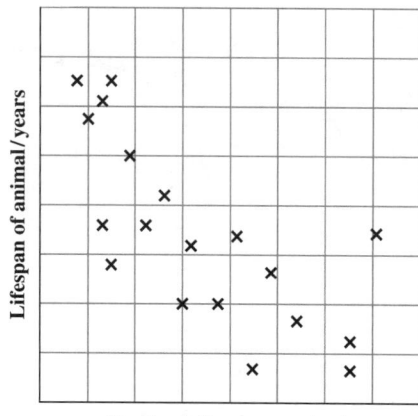

Figure 4.7 Examples of scatter graphs

KEY QUESTIONS TO ASK YOURSELF:

- Is there a correlation between the data points?
- How strong is it?
- What does the correlation show?

The graph in Figure 4.7a suggests that there is a relationship between the lifespan and heart rate. It suggests that as the heart rate of the animal increases its lifespan decreases. This is a negative correlation.

The graph in Figure 4.7b suggests that as the time between heart beats increases, the lifespan of the animal also increases. This is a positive correlation.

Scatter graphs do not show an exact relationship. This is why the data points are scattered – they do not all fall onto a line. The *less scattered* they are, the *stronger* the correlation.

You can draw a best-fit line on a scatter graph to show the general **trend** in the relationship. This could be a straight line or a curve; see Figure 4.8.

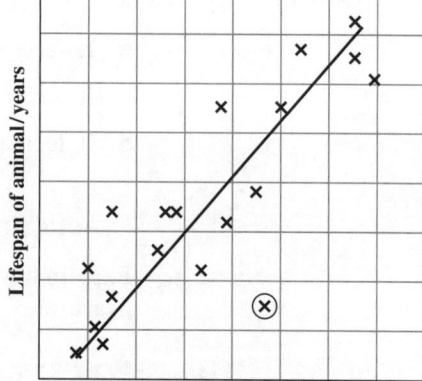

Figure 4.8 A scatter graph with a best-fit line

WATCH OUT

The best-fit line on a scatter graph has a different meaning from the best-fit line on a line graph.

LINK

See Chapter 3, Maths focus 3, Maths skill 3: 'Drawing a line or best-fit curve'.

With a line of best fit on a line graph, the points may not all fit onto the line of best fit because of *errors* in measurement; with a scatter graph, it is because of differences between the *individuals* in the sample.

For example, in Figure 4.8 an *outlier* has been circled. This is away from the best-fit line because this individual mammal has an unusually short lifespan for the time between heart beats; you would expect it to have a longer lifespan to fit the pattern shown by the other mammals. The outlier is not because of an error in measurement.

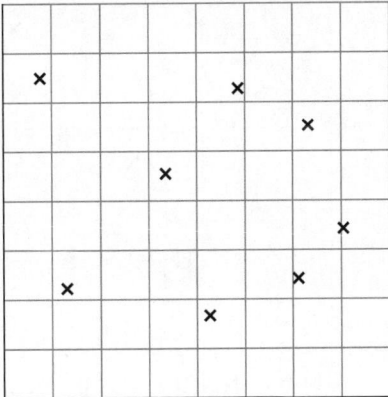

Figure 4.9 A scatter graph showing no correlation between the variables

TIP

If the data points are scattered with no clear correlation, this shows that the two variables are not related, as in Figure 4.9.

Practice question 8

Data were collected from a sample of people.

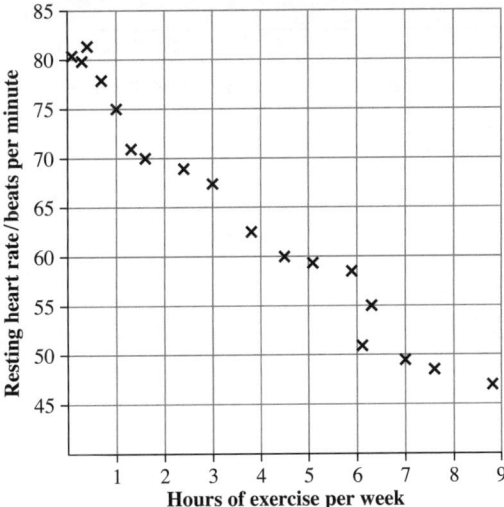

a Draw a best-fit line.

b Describe how strong the correlation is. Give a reason for your answer.

....

....

c Describe what the graph shows.

....

....

71

Practice question 9

The graph shows cigarette consumption (per adult per year) and the number of deaths (per 100 000 people per year) from coronary heart disease (CHD) for 21 countries.

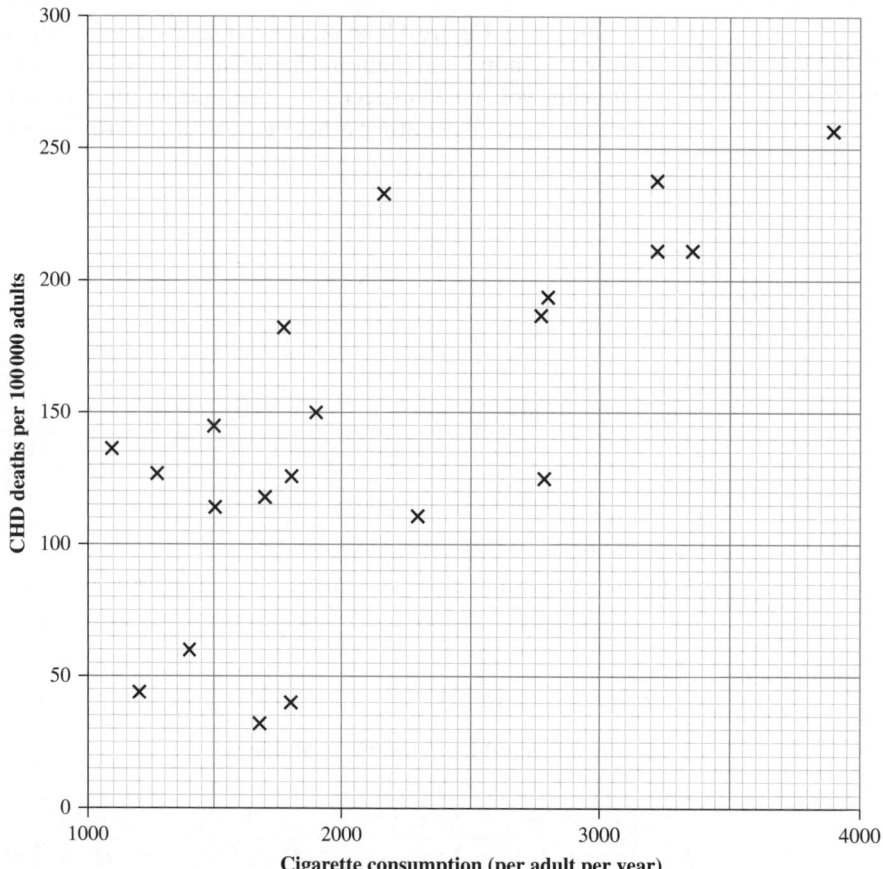

Describe what the graph shows.

....

....

Practice question 10

Scientists collected data on how much saturated fat people ate and the CHD death rate in different European countries.

The graph shows the data.

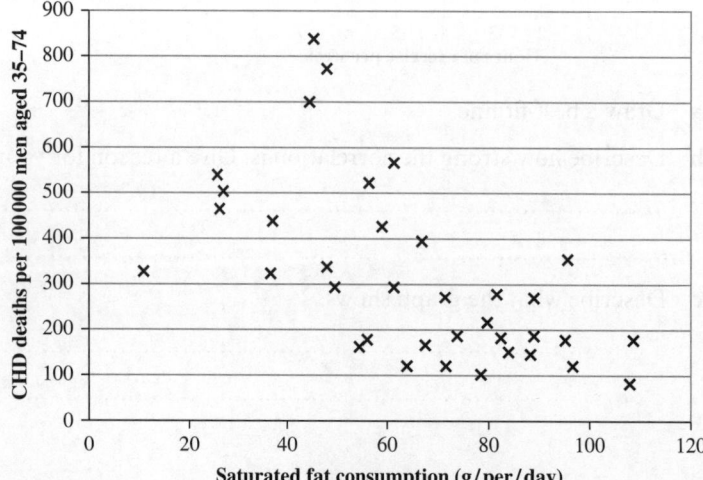

Discuss how well this graph supports the hypothesis that a diet high in saturated fat *does not* increase the risk of developing CHD.

....

....

....

....

....

....

....

Maths focus 3: Reading values from a line graph

Plotting data as a line graph allows you to estimate values between data points. This is called *interpolation*. It is also possible to extend the line and estimate values for higher values. This is called *extrapolation*.

Nitrate solution can be used as a fertiliser, and increase plant growth. A student carried out an investigation to see how increasing the concentration of nitrate solution affected plant growth.

Figure 4.10a shows the graph he plotted from his results and interpolation; Figure 4.10b shows how he could use extrapolation.

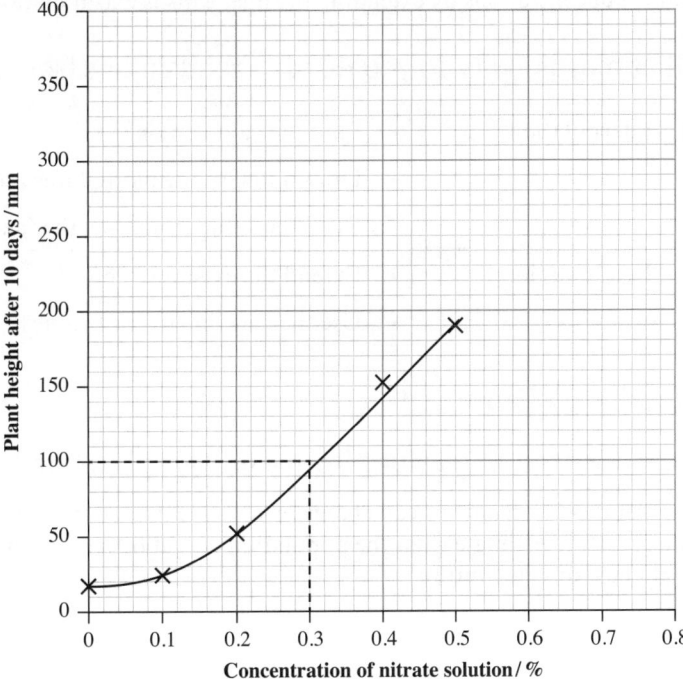

Figure 4.10a Using interpolation

The student did not use a concentration of 0.3%, but he worked out the probable plant height was 100 mm using interpolation.

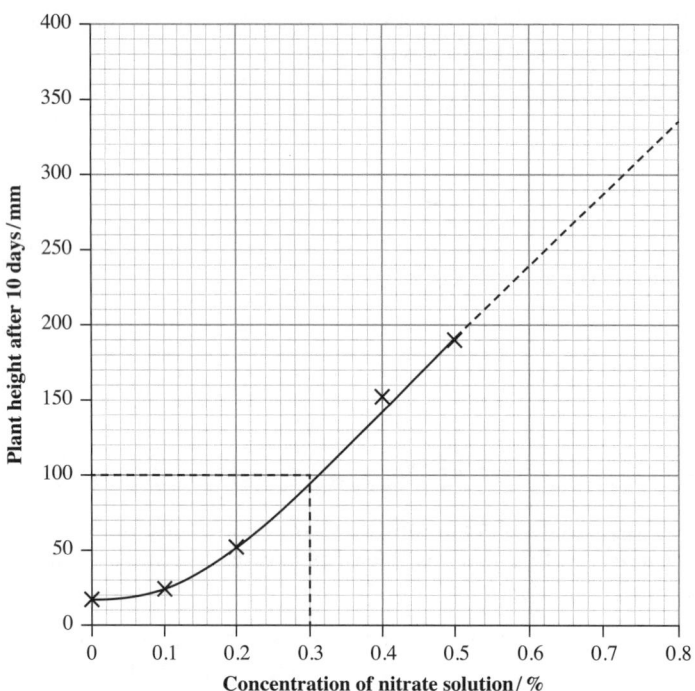

Figure 4.10b Using extrapolation

The highest concentration he used was 0.5%, but he worked out the probable plant height at higher concentrations by extending the line. This is extrapolation.

What maths skills do you need to read values from a line graph?

1 Interpolation	• Find the value on one axis
	• Draw a line to the plotted line and then to the other axis
	• Read the value from the other axis
2 Extrapolation	• Extend the existing line
	• Use the new line to read values

Maths skill practice

How does reading values from a line graph relate to population size?

Populations of organisms can change over time. It is useful to be able to read values from line graphs to estimate what the population was at different times and to also predict what it might be like in the future.

Maths skill 1: Interpolation

WORKED EXAMPLE 6

Figure 4.11 shows the results of an experiment in which yeast cells are added to a container of nutrient broth. The numbers of cells were counted every 6 hours.

The number of yeast cells was measured every 6 hours and a data point plotted. You can work out how many yeast cells there were at any time between 0 and 66 hours by using interpolation.

Work out how many yeast cells there were after 22 hours.

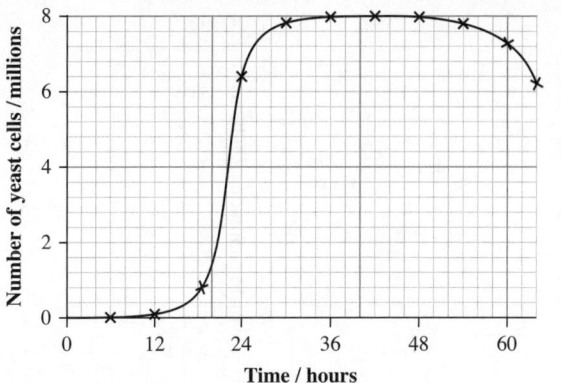

Figure 4.11 The growth of a population of yeast

Step 1: Work out where 22 hours is on the *x*-axis.

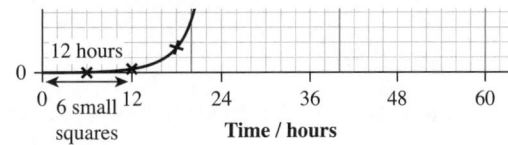

Figure 4.12 How to work out values on an axis

The main division on the *x*-axis is 12 hours. Each main division contains six small squares; see Figure 4.12.

$$12 \div 6 = 2$$

So each small square has a value of 2 hours.

Step 2: Draw a line up from 22 hours until it meets the plotted line.

Step 3: Draw a line to the *y*-axis.

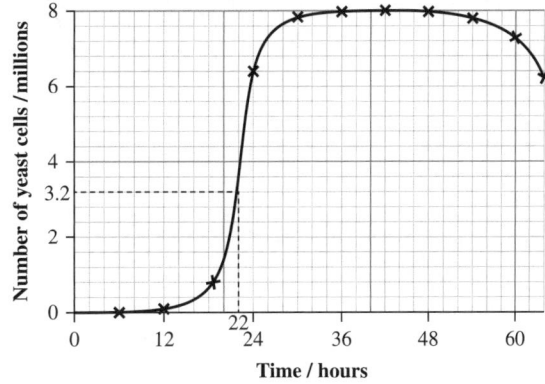

Figure 4.13 How to use interpolation

Step 4: Work out the value on the *y*-axis (see Figure 4.13).

Each main division has a value of 2 and contains five small squares.

$$2 \div 5 = 0.4$$

So, each small square has a value of 0.4 million yeast cells.

The value on the graph is 3.2 million yeast cells.

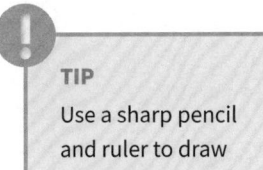

TIP

Use a sharp pencil and ruler to draw the lines.

WATCH OUT

The value worked out by interpolation is an estimate. The more measurements that are made, the more accurate the estimate will be.

Practice question 11

State the value, X, on the graph. ....

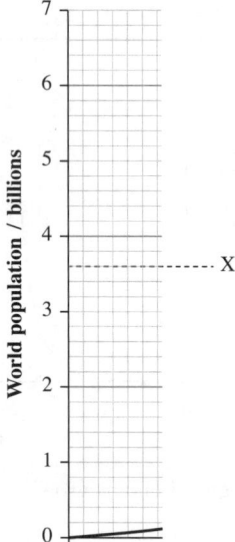

Practice question 12

The graph shows the population growth of a species of bacteria.

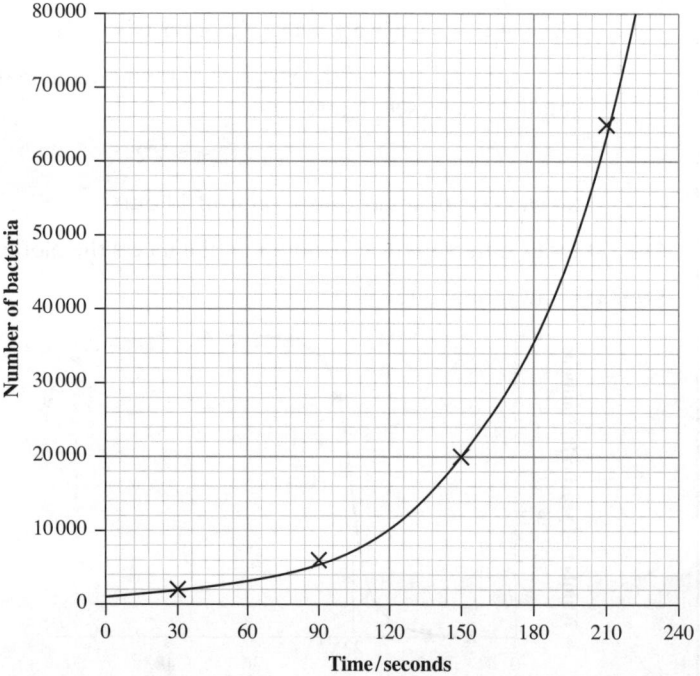

Estimate the number of bacteria after 2 minutes. ....

Practice question 13

The graph shows the growth in numbers of aphids on soya bean plants in a field in North America.

After how many days did the population reach 6000 aphids per plant?

....

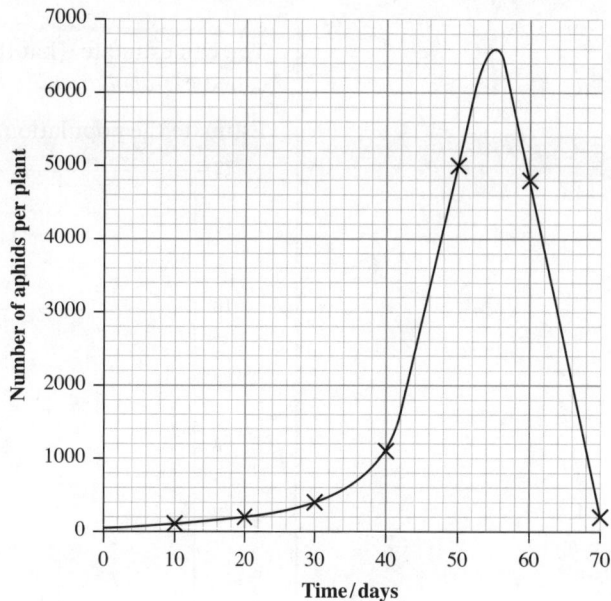

Maths skill 2: Extrapolation

WORKED EXAMPLE 7

Human population has changed over time. Figure 4.14 is a graph that shows this.

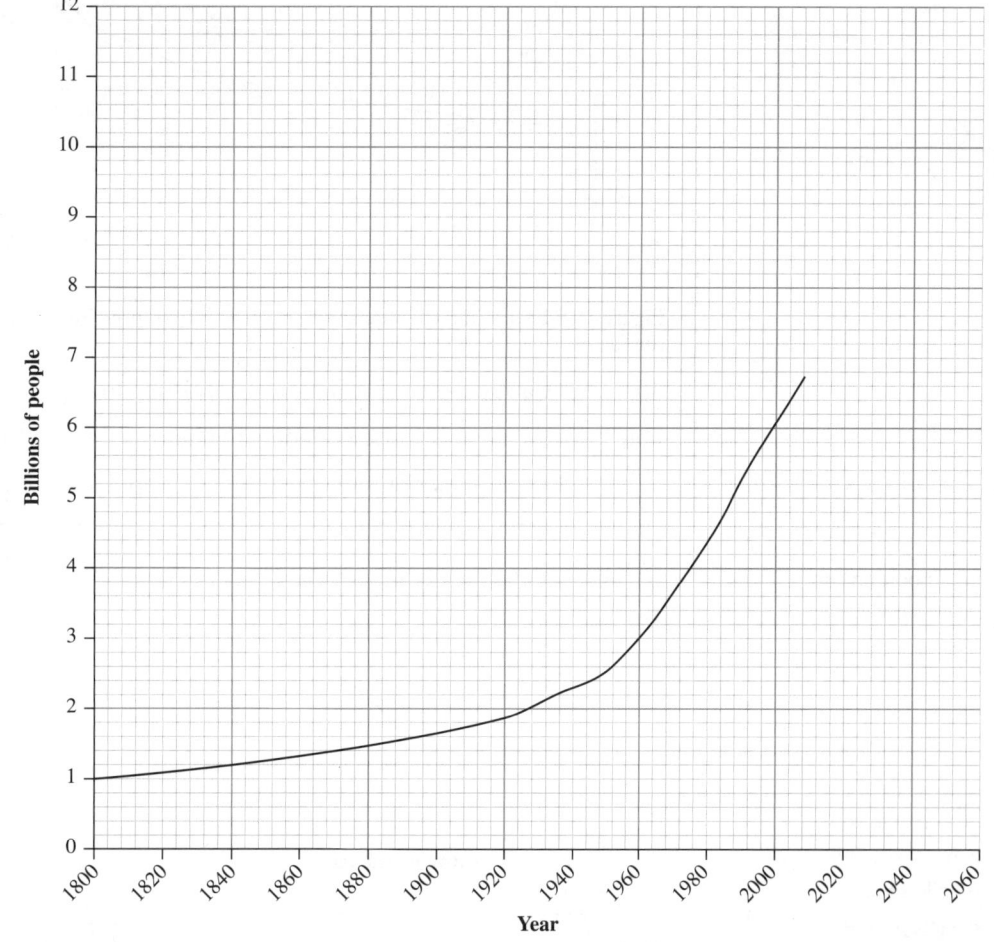

WATCH OUT

Care needs to be taken when using extrapolation. You are assuming that the correlation stays the same outside the data range. This might not always be the case. In Worked Example 7, changes may happen in the future which result in a slower or faster population growth. The estimate is based on assuming that the rate of population change stays the same.

Figure 4.14 The growth of human population on Earth

You can estimate what the population will be in the future by extending the line. This is called *extrapolation*.

Estimate the population by the year 2060.

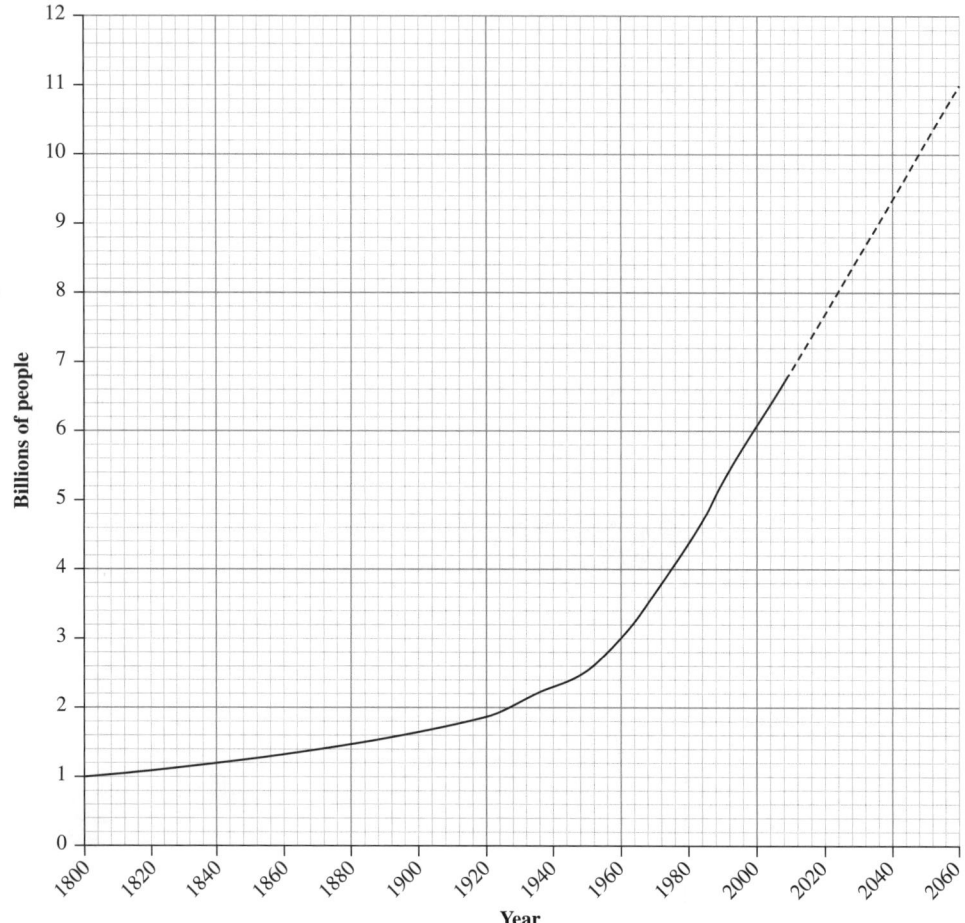

Figure 4.15 Extending the line shows an estimate of how human population will change in the future

Step 1: Use a ruler and place it along the existing line.

Step 2: Draw a new line up, extending the line (see Figure 4.15).

This extrapolation shows that human population could reach 11 billion by 2060.

TIP

Extrapolation can also be used to extend the line towards lower values. You can use this to find out where the line crosses the *x*- or *y*-axis. This is called the **intercept**; see Figure 4.16.

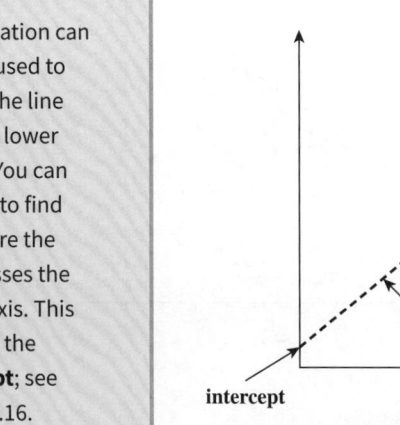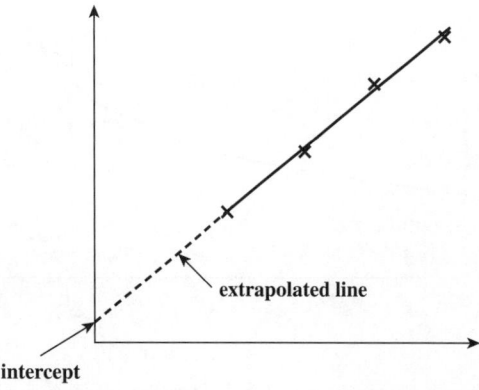

Figure 4.16 Extrapolation by extending the line towards lower values

Practice question 14

Use a ruler to extrapolate these lines:

a to higher values   **b** to higher values   **c** to lower values

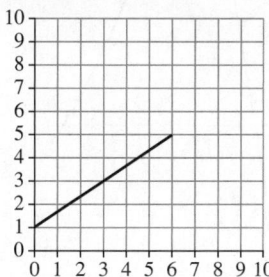 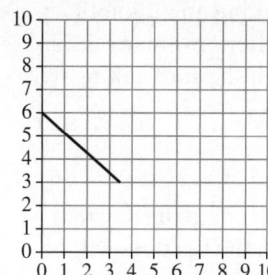 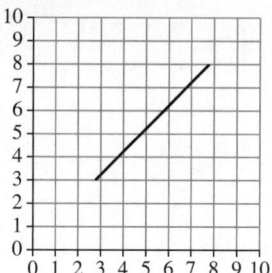

Practice question 15

A population of flamingos live in a safari park.

The graph shows how their population has changed.

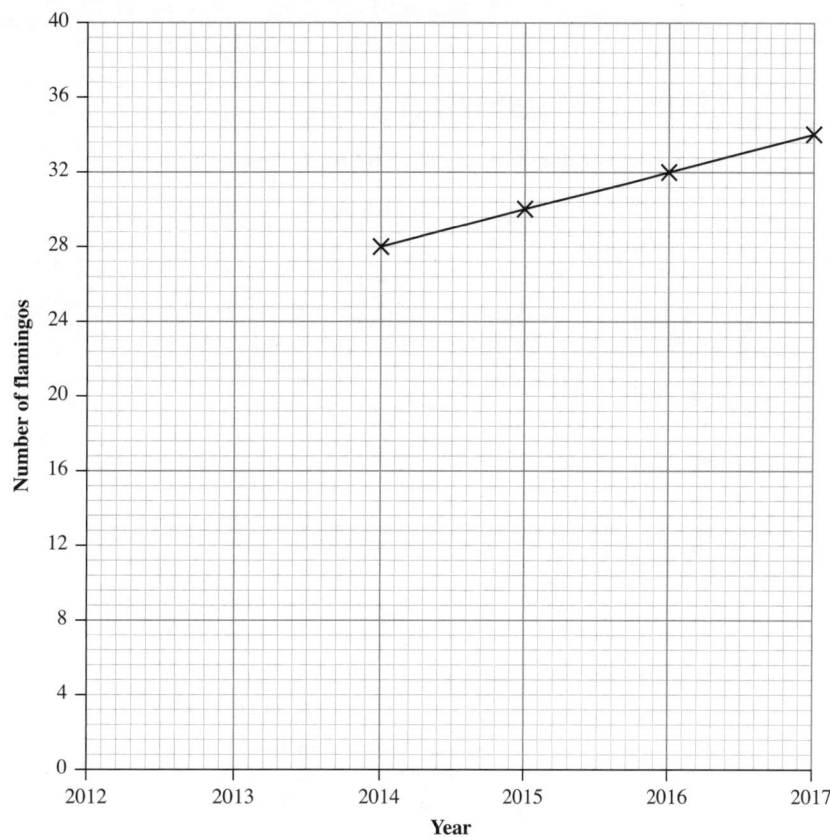

Use the graph to estimate the number of flamingos in the park in 2012.

....

Practice question 16

A patient has a bacterial infection. The graph shows how the population of bacteria changed.

a The patient started taking an antibiotic. After how many days did she start taking it?

....

....

b Estimate the day that all the bacteria will be killed.

....

....

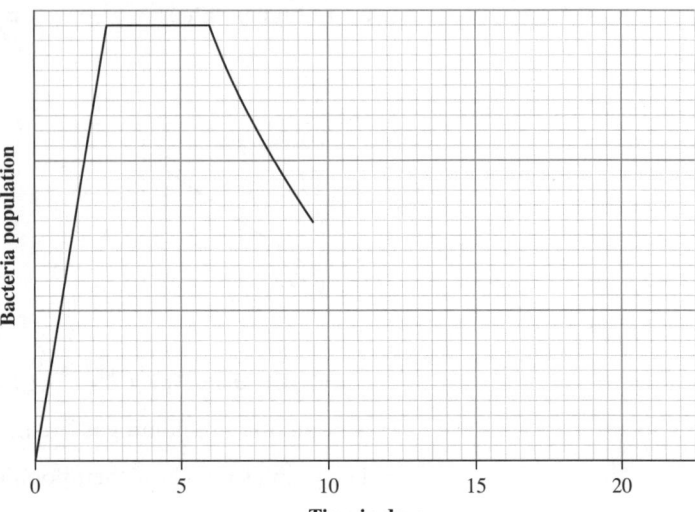

Further question

A student was asked to cycle on an exercise bicycle.

The graph shows how his breathing rate changed.

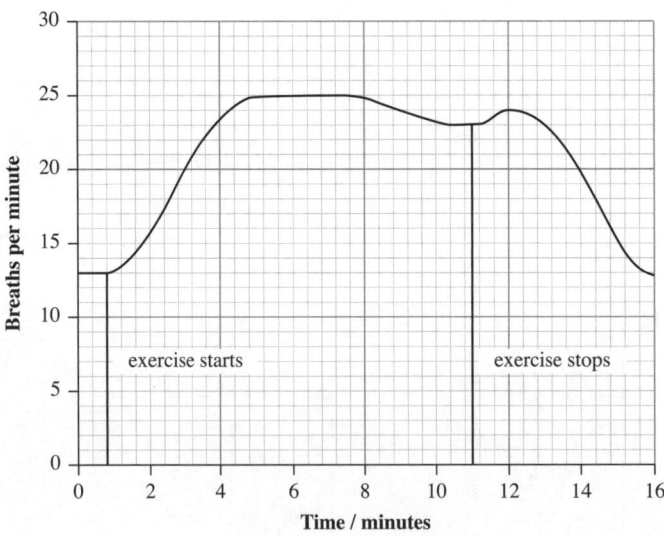

a State how long the student was exercising for.

....

b Calculate the increase in breathing rate from when the student started exercising to the maximum rate.

....

c Describe what happened to the change in breathing rate in the final 3 minutes of exercise. Suggest a reason for this change.

....

....

Why do you need to do calculations in biology?

- You will be presented with information in various different forms including data and diagrams.
- Doing calculations, such as calculating percentages, ratios and scale, will help you to interpret the information.

Maths focus 1: Calculating percentages

The term 'per cent' means one out of a hundred. The symbol % is used to denote a **percentage**.

Some examples of percentages being used in biology are:

- Of all the species that have existed on Earth, 99.9% are now extinct.
- Humans share 50% of their DNA with bananas.
- Around 10% of people are left-handed.

We can use percentages to estimate proportions.

For example, if 10% of people are left-handed then in a population of 50 million people, we would expect 5 million to be left-handed.

An important part of biology is studying change. This might be a change in the mass of an organism, or a change in a variable during an investigation. Calculating percentage increase or decrease gives a value about how much this value has changed.

What maths skills do you need to calculate percentages?

1 Calculating percentages	• Calculate the percentage of a quantity, e.g. 40% of 50
	• Calculate a quantity as a percentage, e.g. 18 out of 72
2 Calculating percentage change	• Calculate the difference between the numbers you are comparing:
	$$\text{Difference} = \text{new number} - \text{original number}$$
	• Divide the difference by the original number and multiply the number by 100:
	$$\% \text{ change} = \left(\frac{\text{difference}}{\text{original number}}\right) \times 100$$
	• Decide if it shows a percentage increase or decrease

Maths skill practice

How does calculating percentages relate to organisms and their environment?

The study of organisms and how they interact with their environment is called *ecology*.

Animals (*consumers*) get the energy they need to live by eating. You can calculate how much of the energy in the food they eat is used for different life processes as a percentage.

The size of a population can change over time, as shown in Figure 5.1. Calculating the percentage decrease or increase will allow you to see how much the population has changed by compared to previous years.

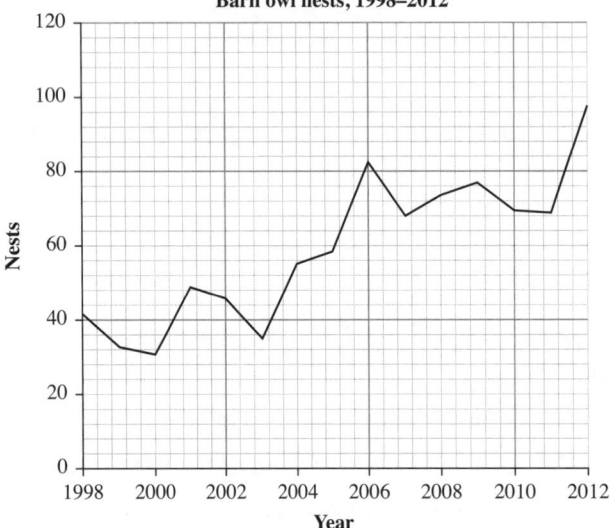

Barn owl nests, 1998–2012

Figure 5.1 The number of barn owl nests changes over time. Can you see between which years there was a population increase and which years there was a decrease?

Maths skill 1: Calculating percentages

WORKED EXAMPLE 1

Some locusts ate some maize.

The maize contained 5000 kJ of energy.

Only 10% of this energy was passed to the locusts.

Calculate the amount of energy transferred to the locusts.

This question is asking you to calculating the *percentage* of a quantity.

Step 1: Change the percentage to a decimal by dividing it by 100:

$$\frac{10}{100} = 0.1$$

Step 2: Multiply by the quantity:

$$0.1 \times 5000 = 500 \,\text{kJ}$$

The answer is 500 kJ.

LINK

For more information about place value, refer to Chapter 1, Maths focus 2, 'Representing very large and very small values'.

WORKED EXAMPLE 2

Figure 5.2 shows how a caterpillar transfers energy from its food.

Calculate the percentage of food used for growth.

Food 20 J ⟶
Respiration 6 J
Growth 3 J
Faeces 11 J

Figure 5.2 How a caterpillar transfers energy from its food

The question is asking you to calculate a *quantity as a percentage*.

Step 1: Identify the two numbers you need to use.

This is the amount of energy in food and the amount of energy used for growth.

So, you need to use the numbers 20 and 3.

Step 2: Divide the smaller number by the larger number.

$$\frac{3}{20} = 0.15$$

Step 3: Multiply the answer by 100.

$$0.15 \times 100 = 15\%$$

The percentage of food used for growth is 15%.

Practice question 1

Calculate:

a 20% of 240 ....

b 12% of 360 ....

c 75% of 1520 ....

Practice question 2

Use Figure 5.2 to calculate the percentage of energy from food that a caterpillar loses in its faeces.

....

Practice question 3

A student has a bird table in her garden.

She uses a tally chart to count how many birds of each species visit the bird table in 1 hour.

Her results are shown in the following table.

Bird species	Visits in 1 hour
Common redstart	|||
Red-vented bulbul		
Whinchat	|||| ||
Isabelline wheatear	||

a Calculate the total number of birds that she sees.

....

b What percentage of the birds was a common redstart?

....

Maths skill 2: Calculating percentage change

WORKED EXAMPLE 3

Table 5.1 shows how the herring population in the North Sea has changed between 1965 and 2005.

Year	Herring biomass / thousand tonnes
1965	2035
1970	452
1975	149
1980	105
1985	743
1990	1256
1995	502
2000	954
2005	1928

Table 5.1 Change in the herring population in the North Sea

Calculate the percentage change in herring biomass between 1965 and 1970.

State if it is a percentage increase or decrease.

In 1965 the herring biomass was 2035 thousand tonnes. In 1970 it was 452 thousand tonnes.

Step 1: Calculate the difference between the numbers you are comparing:

$$\text{Difference} = \text{new number} - \text{original number}$$

$$452 - 2035 = -1583$$

TIP

Because both numbers show thousand tonnes, you can just use the numbers 2035 and 452 in your calculation.

Step 2: Divide the difference by the original number and multiply the number by 100:

$$\% \text{ change} = \left(\frac{\text{difference}}{\text{original number}}\right) \times 100$$

$$\left(\frac{-1583}{2035}\right) \times 100 = -77.8\%$$

Step 3: Decide if your answer shows a percentage increase or decrease.

The answer is a negative number which is a percentage decrease.

The answer is a 77.8% decrease in herring biomass between 1965 and 1970.

Practice question 4

Use Table 5.1 to calculate the percentage change in the biomass of herring population between 2000 and 2005.

Give your answer to one decimal place.

State if it is a percentage increase or decrease.

....

....

....

Practice question 5

Figure 5.3 shows the amount of energy in the tissues of organisms in a food chain.

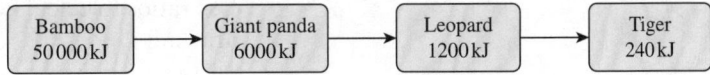

Figure 5.3 The amount of energy along a food chain

Calculate the percentage energy loss between:

a Bamboo and giant panda

....

....

....

b Giant panda and leopard

....

....

....

c Leopard and tiger

....

....

....

WATCH OUT

You might come across ratios on scale drawings. These are rarely used in biology, but you might use them in other subjects.

In Figure 5.4, the scale ratio is 1:40. This means that 1 unit of length on the drawing is equal to 40 units on the actual horse. So, 1 cm on the drawing is equal to 40 cm on the actual horse.

Maths focus 2: Using scale drawings and magnification

In biology you will often have to study objects that are very small, such as cells, and very large, such as entire habitats.

These objects are drawn as **scale drawings**, which makes them a suitable size to be displayed on the page of a book or a computer screen.

In order to calculate the *actual size* of an object, a **scale** is used, which tells you the ratio of any length in the drawing to the corresponding length in the actual object.

Figure 5.4 shows an example of a scale drawing.

400 mm
←→

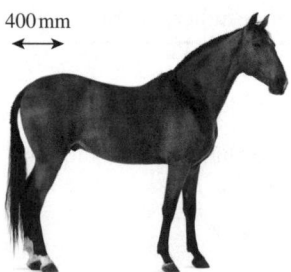

Figure 5.4 A scale drawing of a horse

What maths skills do you need to use scale?

1	Interpreting scale drawings	• Use a ruler to measure the length of the scale bar given in the drawing
		• Use a ruler to measure the drawing
		• Use ratios to calculate the actual size of the drawing
		• Use the correct unit in the answer
2	Using the magnification formula	• Identify the magnification (it will start with a ×)
		• Use a ruler to measure the image in millimetres
		• Use the formula: $$\text{real size} = \frac{\text{size of the image}}{\text{magnification}}$$

LINK

See Chapter 1, Maths focus 1, 'Using units', for information on how to convert units.

Maths skill practice

How does using scale relate to cells?

Cells are very small. They are microscopic – this means that to view them you need a microscope to magnify them.

A typical human skin cell has a diameter of 30 μm, or 0.03 mm.

The images of cells that you see in books are enlarged images. They are often scale drawings, so the actual size of the cell can be calculated.

Some scale drawings will provide you with a scale bar (as in Figure 5.5a). Others will have a **magnification** (as in Figure 5.5b). Both will allow you to calculate the actual size of the cell.

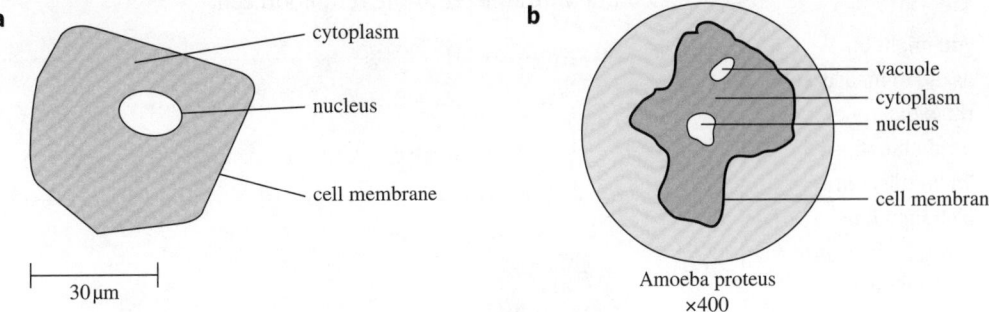

Figure 5.5 Scale drawings of cells

Maths skill 1: Interpreting scale drawings

WORKED EXAMPLE 4

A student found a diagram of a bacterium in her course book, as shown in Figure 5.6.

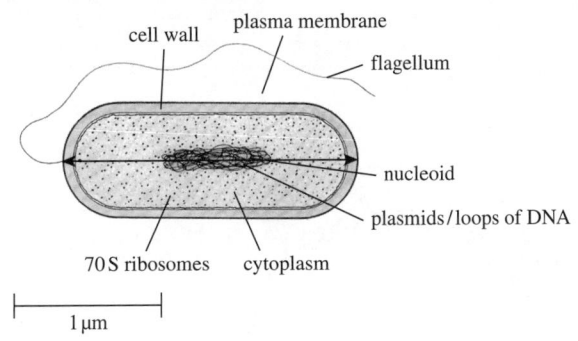

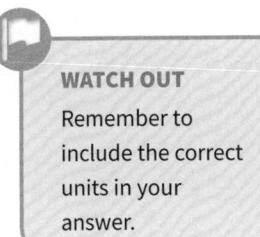

WATCH OUT

Remember to include the correct units in your answer.

Figure 5.6 A bacterium

What is the length of the bacterium (not including the flagellum)?

Step 1: Measure the length of the scale bar.

The scale line is 2 cm long.

This means that 2 cm on the diagram represents 1 μm.

Step 2: Measure the drawing.

The length of the bacterium in the drawing is 4 cm.

Step 3: Use ratios to calculate the actual size of the drawing.

	Size on drawing	**Real size**
Scale bar:	2 cm ⎞ ×2	1 μm ⎞ ×2
Length of bacterium:	4 cm ⎠	? ⎠

So, the length of the bacterium (not including the flagellum) is 2 μm.

87

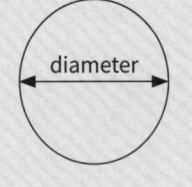

TIP

You might be asked to measure the *diameter* of a circular object. To do this, draw a straight line through the centre of the object.

diameter

Practice question 6

Calculate the diameter of the red blood cell.

....

....

....

....

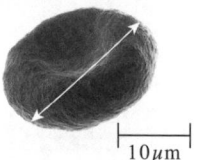

$10\,\mu m$

Practice question 7

Calculate the diameter of the virus in the scale drawing.

....

....

....

....

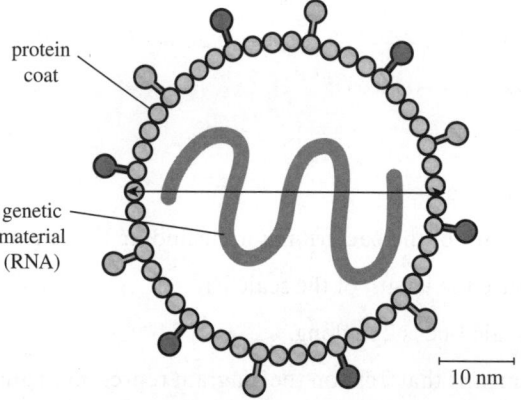

protein coat

genetic material (RNA)

10 nm

Maths skill 2: Using the magnification formula

The magnification formula is:

$$\text{real size} = \frac{\text{size of the image}}{\text{magnification}}$$

This formula can be used to calculate the real size of an object, such as a cell, using the size of a magnified image.

The magnification will be given on the image.

The form of the equation used to calculate the magnification is:

$$\text{magnification} = \frac{\text{size of the image}}{\text{real size}}$$

WATCH OUT

A magnification of × 10 000 tells you that in the image the object has been magnified by 10 000; it is 10 000 times bigger than in real life.

TIP

Magnification is a *ratio* of two lengths so it has no unit.

TIP

The answer is given to two significant figures, but the conversion gives three. 38 mm is two significant figures.

LINK

See Chapter 1, 'Representing values' for more information on significant figures.

WORKED EXAMPLE 5

Figure 5.7 shows cells from the trachea (windpipe) of a mammal.

Use the magnification formula to calculate the length of the cell marked in the image.

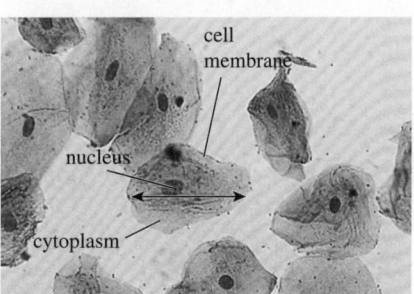

Figure 5.7 Cells from the trachea (windpipe) of a mammal, seen through a light microscope (× 300)

Step 1: Identify the magnification (it will start with ×)

The magnification is × 300. This means that the image is 300 times larger than the real cells.

Step 2: Use a ruler to measure the image in millimetres.

The length of the marked cell is 16 mm.

Step 3: Use the formula:

$$\text{real size} = \frac{\text{size of the image}}{\text{magnification}}$$

$$\text{real size} = \frac{16\,\text{mm}}{300}$$

$$= 0.05\,\text{mm}$$

The real size of the marked cell is 0.05 mm.

You need to convert mm into μm (micrometres):

$$1000\,\mu\text{m} = 1\,\text{mm}$$

$$\text{So, } 0.05\,\text{mm} = 50\,\mu\text{m}$$

Practice question 8

The following image is a close-up of leaf cells. It has a magnification of × 2000.

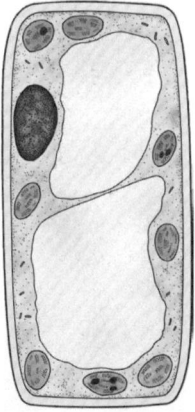

Calculate the height of the cell in millimetres.

Use the magnification formula.

....

....

....

Practice question 9

The following image is part of a liver cell, taken using an electron microscope.

The magnification is × 20 000.

Calculate the diameter of the nucleus in micrometres (μm).

Use the magnification formula.

....

....

....

Practice question 10

A drawing of a plant cell in a textbook has a length of 10.2 cm.

The actual plant cell has a length of 0.1 mm.

Use the formula to calculate the magnification of the image.

$$\text{magnification} = \frac{\text{size of the image}}{\text{real size}}$$

....

....

....

Practice question 11

A student found an electron microscope image of a mitochondrion.

The width of the mitochondrion in the image was 34 mm.

The width of a real mitochondrion is 1 μm.

Use the magnification formula to calculate the magnification of the image.

....

....

....

Maths focus 3: Understanding ratio and probability

Ratios are used in everyday life to compare amounts of something. For example, in a recipe it says to use 2 parts flour to 1 part cocoa. This means that you need to use twice as much flour compared to cocoa. This could be 50 g of flour and 25 g of cocoa or 200 g of flour and 100 g of cocoa.

In biology a scientist can use ratio and probability in genetic experiments.

For example:

A scientist grew 10 pea plants from seeds.

Six of the pea plants had white flowers.

The other four had pink flowers.

He can discuss the results in terms of:

Ratio: The ratio of white to pink flowers is 6 : 4. This can be simplified to 3 : 2.

Probability: If he had picked a seed at random and planted it, there would have been a 6 in 10, or 60%, chance that the plant will have white flowers and a 4 in 10, or 40%, chance that it will have pink flowers.

What maths skills do you need to calculate ratio and probability?

1	Calculating ratio	• Read the ratio you need to calculate, e.g. number of A to the number of B
		• Write the amounts with a colon : in between them. Put the numbers in the correct order so A will go first.
		• Write the ratio in its simplest form
2	Calculating probability	• Work out the number of possible outcomes. This is y
		• Work out the number of outcomes of interest. This is x
		• Give the probability in the form of x in y
		• Simplify the probability if possible

Maths skill practice

How does calculating ratio and probability relate to inheritance?

Offspring produced by sexual reproduction share features with both parents.

This happens because chromosomes are passed from parent to offspring.

Genetic diagrams, like the *Punnett square* in Figure 5.8, show the alleles of each parent (their *genotypes*) plus all the possible combinations that can be produced in the offspring. You can use genetic diagrams to calculate the ratio and probability of different genotypes and phenotypes.

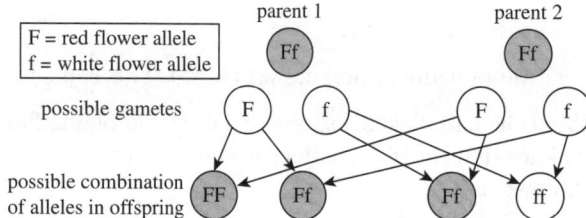

(Female) eggs

		G	g
Male (sperm)	G	GG *Grey*	Gg *Grey*
	g	Gg *Grey*	gg *Black*

Figure 5.8 A Punnett square which shows the possible combinations of alleles from two parent cats

The phenotype is fur colour, which can be grey or black.

Maths skill 1: Calculating ratio

A *ratio* is a way of comparing amounts of something.

TIP

The Punnett square in Figure 5.8 shows that there are four possible combinations of alleles. Three of these result in the phenotype grey fur, and one results in black fur.

TIP

To simplify the ratio, first work out the largest number that each amount in the ratio is divisible by. Then, divide each amount by this number.

TIP

When you read a ratio say 'to' for the colon (:). So, for this ratio you say 'three to one'.

WATCH OUT

The largest amount is not always written first. If the question asked for the ratio of white to red flowers, then the answer would be 1:3.

WORKED EXAMPLE 6

Figure 5.9 is a genetic diagram that a student found in a textbook.

It shows how flower colour is inherited in pea plants.

F = red flower allele
f = white flower allele

parent 1   Ff   parent 2   Ff

possible gametes   F   f   F   f

possible combination of alleles in offspring   FF   Ff   Ff   ff

Figure 5.9 A genetic diagram showing alleles for red and white flowers

What is the ratio of possible combinations of alleles in offspring of:

a red to white flowers

b homozygous to heterozygous genotypes?

Part a: Here are the steps you should take:

Step 1: Read the ratio you need to calculate, e.g. number of A to the number of B.

Part **a** asks for the ratio of red to white flowers.

Three of the combinations result in red flowers, and one in white flowers.

Step 2: Write the amounts with a : in between them. Put the numbers in the correct order so A will go first.

3:1

Step 3: Write the ratio in its simplest form.

The largest number both amounts can be divided by is 1, so 3:1 is the simplest form of the ratio.

The ratio of red to white flowers is 3:1. This is called the *phenotypic ratio*.

This ratio shows there are three red flowers to every one white flower.

Part b: Two of the combinations have a *homozygous genotype* (FF or ff) and two have a *heterozygous genotype* (Ff).

The ratio of homozygous genotype to heterozygous is 2:2.

Both sides of the ratio are divisible by 2, so it can be simplified to give a ratio of 1:1.

This ratio shows that there are an equal number of homozygous and heterozygous genotypes in the combinations.

Practice question 12

a A litter of kittens contains three with short hair and two with long hair. What is the ratio of short to long haired kittens?

....

b In a group of 10 fruit flies, seven have red eyes and the rest have white eyes. Write this as a ratio of red eyes to white eyes.

....

Practice question 13

Simplify these ratios:

a 10:5

....

b 4:16

....

c 9:3

....

d 40:120

....

Practice question 14

The following genetic diagram shows a cross between two cats.

Female (eggs)

Male (sperm)		g	g
	G	Gg *Grey fur*	Gg *Grey fur*
	g	gg *Black fur*	gg *Black fur*

What is the expected ratio of grey to black fur in the offspring?

....

Maths skill 2: Calculating probability

Probability shows how likely it is that an event will occur.

If you toss a coin, then there are two possible outcomes – heads or tails.

Each time you toss a coin the probability of getting a head is 1 in 2. The probability of getting a tail is also 1 in 2.

Genetic diagrams show us all the possible combinations of alleles that can form in the offspring. Probability can be used to show how likely the different combinations are.

TIP

In the genetic diagrams you will use, there will always be a total of *four* possible combinations.

TIP

Probability can also be shown as a percentage, fraction or decimal number. For example, 1 in 2 can also be written as 50%, $\frac{1}{2}$ or 0.5.

WATCH OUT

These probabilities show the *likelihood* of each phenotype each time the parents have a baby. It does *not* show the exact numbers. For example, if the parents had four children then we might expect one baby to have cystic fibrosis, but in reality it could be none or more than one.

WORKED EXAMPLE 7

Cystic fibrosis (cf) is a genetic illness caused by two recessive alleles, aa.

Figure 5.10 is a genetic diagram that shows the cross between two parents who are carriers for cystic fibrosis.

		Female (eggs)	
		A	a
Male (sperm)	A	AA *Do not have cf*	Aa *Carrier of cf*
	a	Aa *Carrier of cf*	aa *Have cf*

Figure 5.10 A genetic cross to show the possible combination of alleles from two parents who are carriers of cystic fibrosis

What is the probability that a child born from the parents above will:

a have cystic fibrosis

b not have cystic fibrosis

c be a carrier of cystic fibrosis

d not have cystic fibrosis or be a carrier?

a The genotype for this phenotype is aa. There is one aa in the cross.

Probability = 1 in 4

b The genotypes for this phenotype are AA and Aa.

Probability = 3 in 4

c The genotype for this phenotype is Aa.

Probability = 2 in 4

Both numbers can be divided by 2 so this is simplified to 1 in 2.

d The genotype for this phenotype is AA

Probability = 1 in 4

Practice question 15

Huntington's disease is an example of a genetic illness. If you have the dominant allele, H, you have the illness.

The following genetic cross shows the possible outcomes from a woman who has the disease and a man who does not.

		Female (eggs)	
		H	h
Male (sperm)	h	Hh *Has illness*	hh *Healthy*
	h	Hh *Has illness*	hh *Healthy*

a Calculate the probability of the couple having a child with the illness.

Give your answer as a percentage.

....

b What would the probability be if the woman has the genotype HH?

....

Practice question 16

Sex is inherited through sex chromosomes, X and Y.

Females have two **XX** sex chromosomes and males have **XY** chromosomes.

Use the following genetic cross to show why the probability of having a baby boy is 1 in 2.

		Female (eggs)	
		X	X
Male (sperm)	X	XX	XX
	Y	XY	XY

....

....

Further questions

1 The image of the cheek cell shown has a magnification of × 100.

The width of the cell is shown by the line.

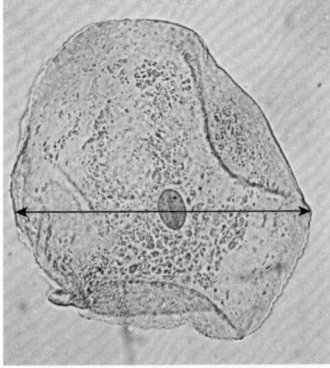

a Calculate the real size of the cell in millimetres.

Use the formula:

$$\text{real size} = \frac{\text{size of the image}}{\text{magnification}}$$

....

....

b Convert this width into micrometres (μm).

....

....

c A red blood cell has a diameter of 8 μm.

A bacterial cell is 40 times smaller.

Calculate the diameter of a bacterial cell.

....

2 Blood is a tissue made up of many different components.

The diagram shows the percentage of each component, by volume, in a sample of blood.

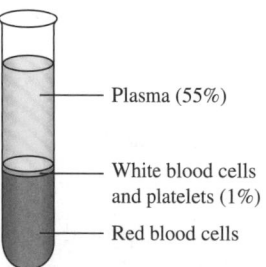

Plasma (55%)

White blood cells
and platelets (1%)

Red blood cells

a Calculate the volume of plasma in a 156 cm³ sample of blood.

....

....

b The table shows the number of the different blood cells per microlitre (μl) in a sample of blood.

Blood component	Number per μl
platelets	250 000
neutrophils	3000
lymphocytes	100
monocytes	150
basophils	25
red blood cells	5 000 000

Calculate the ratio of red blood cells to platelets.

....

....

....

Chapter 6

Working with shape

Why do you need to work with shape in biology?

- Some of the two-dimensional (2D) shapes you will come across in biology are squares, rectangles and circles.
- The area of a shape is often used in calculations.

Maths focus: Calculating area

Area is a measurement of the surface of an object.

In biology you will need to be able to calculate the area of rectangles and squares as well as circles.

What maths skills do you need to calculate area?

1	Calculating the area of a rectangle or square	• **Square:** multiply the length of a side by itself
		• **Rectangle:** multiply the length of a long side by the length of a short side
2	Calculating the area of a circle	• The formula used is: area = πr^2
		• Use a ruler to measure the radius of the circle
		• Square the radius (multiply it by itself)
		• Multiply the radius by π

Maths skill practice

How does calculating area relate to investigations in biology?

Circles

The area of circles are calculated when looking at how effective different chemicals, such as antibiotics, are against bacteria.

The bacteria are grown on agar in a Petri dish and small discs that have been soaked in the antibiotic are placed on the agar. After the bacteria have grown, there will be clear circular regions around the effective antibiotics (see Figure 6.2). The area of these regions (called *zones of inhibition*) can be calculated to find out which antibiotic was the most effective: the larger the area of the circle, the more effective the antibiotic.

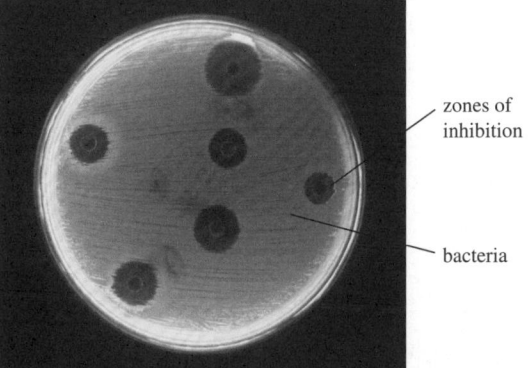

zones of inhibition

bacteria

Figure 6.2 The antibiotics diffuse from the paper discs and prevent bacteria from growing. This forms circular zones of inhibition

Squares (Extention)

Quadrats are square frames that are used in sampling plants or slow moving animals, such as snails.

The quadrat is placed randomly on the ground in the habitat, as shown in Figure 6.1. The number of organisms inside the quadrat is counted. The area of the whole *habitat* is calculated so the number of organisms in the quadrat can be used to estimate the number in the whole habitat.

Figure 6.1 This quadrat has been divided into smaller squares to make counting the plants easier. Each side of the quadrat is 50 cm long

Maths skill 1: Calculating the area of a rectangle or square

The area of both a square and a rectangle is calculated by multiplying the length of their sides.

For a square: Multiply the length of a side by itself, $a \times a$ or a^2; see Figure 6.3.

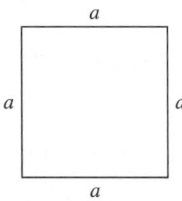

Figure 6.3 The area of a square is $a \times a$

For a rectangle: Multiply the length of a long side by the length of a short side, $a \times b$; see Figure 6.4.

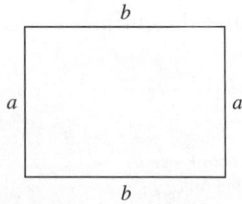

Figure 6.4 The area of a rectangle is $a \times b$

TIP

The **surface area** of a three-dimensional (3D) shape can be calculated by adding up the area of its sides.

A cube has six sides; see Figure 6.5. So, a cube with a side length of 1 cm will have a surface area of 6 cm².

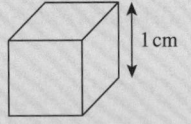

Figure 6.5 This cube will have a surface area of 6 cm²

LINK

You can find out more about units in Chapter 1, 'Representing values'.

Common units of length used in biology are mm, cm, m and km.

The corresponding units of area are mm^2, cm^2, m^2 and km^2.

Many students make the same mistake when converting units of area.

For example, they may think that $1\,cm^2$ is equal to $10\,mm^2$ because $1\,cm = 10\,mm$.

However, as you can see in Figure 6.6, this is not correct. A square with a side of $1\,cm$ contains 100 (10×10) squares with a side of $1\,mm$. So, $1\,cm^2 = 100\,mm^2$.

To convert the units of area you must square the *multiplier* used for the conversion of length:

$$mm \rightarrow cm \; (\times 10)$$

$$mm^2 \rightarrow cm^2 \; (\times 10^2)$$

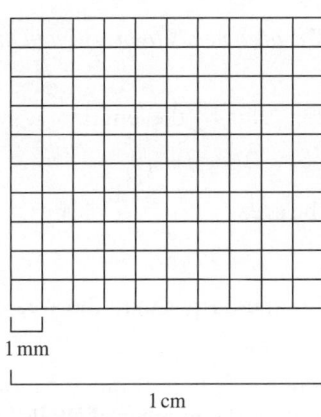

1 mm

1 cm

Figure 6.6 An area of $1\,cm^2$ equals $100\,mm^2$

WORKED EXAMPLE 1 (EXTENTION)

A student investigated how many snails were living in an area of the school field.

She used a quadrat with sides measuring 50cm.

Figure 6.7 shows the size of the field she sampled.

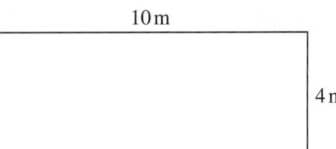

10 m

4 m

Figure 6.7 The school field

Calculate the area in m^2 of the:

a quadrat

b field

Part **a**, the quadrat:

Step 1: Decide if the shape is a square or a rectangle.

The sides of the quadrat are all 50cm, so the quadrat is a square.

Step 2: Make sure the units of length are correct. If not, convert them.

The sides are 50 cm long. The area needs to be given in m².

$$50\,cm = \frac{50}{100} = 0.5\,m$$

WATCH OUT

Make sure that the units of length for each side are the same.

TIP

It is easier to convert the units of length, rather than area, so convert the length first before calculating the area.

Step 3: Calculate area by squaring the length of one side.

$$0.5^2 = 0.25$$

Step 4: Use the correct unit for the area.

$$0.25\,m^2$$

Part **b**, the field:

Step 1: Decide if the shape is a square or a rectangle.

The field is a rectangle.

Step 2: Make sure the units of length are correct. If not, convert them.

The sides are in metres. The area needs to be given in m^2 so no conversion is needed.

Step 3: Multiply the length of a long side by the length of a short side

$$10 \times 4 = 40$$

Step 4: Use the correct unit for the area.

$$40\,m^2$$

The area of the field is 160 times larger than the area of the quadrat. $(40 \div 0.25 = 160)$.

This means that the student needs to multiply the number of snails counted in one quadrat by 160 to estimate the number of snails in the whole field.

Practice question 1

a The length of the sides of a quadrat is 25 cm.

Calculate the area in cm².

....

b A square field has an area of 4 km².

i Calculate the length of one side.

....

ii Calculate the area in m².

....

Practice question 2

The diagram shows part of a beach.

Calculate the area.

....

....

....

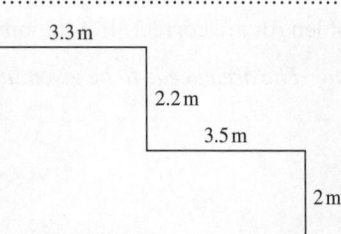

Practice question 3 (Extention)

A student used a quadrat with sides of 50 cm to sample a rectangular area of land with lengths of 5.2 m and 12.8 m.

How many times larger was the area of the land compared to the quadrat?

....

....

....

Practice question 4

A student was investigating osmosis. He cut pieces of potato into rectangular blocks, as shown in the diagram.

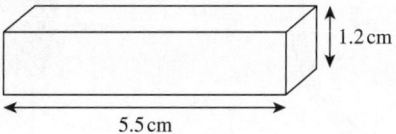

Calculate the surface area of the block.

....

....

....

Maths skill 2: Calculating the area of a circle

The formula used to calculate the area of a circle is:

$$\text{area} = \pi \times \text{radius}^2$$

This can be shortened to: $A = \pi r^2$

See Figure 6.8 for the parts of a circle: **radius**, **diameter** and **circumference**.

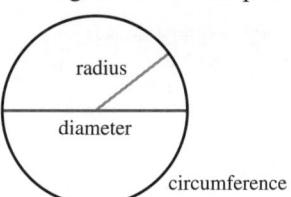

Figure 6.8 The radius is the distance between the centre of the circle and the circumference

π is the symbol for the Greek letter pi. It is pronounced 'pie'. It is 3.14 to three significant figures.

TIP

You will have a π button on your calculator which gives you the number not rounded up. Use this in calculations to give a more accurate answer.

WORKED EXAMPLE 2

A scientist wanted to see which antibiotic was most effective against a strain of bacteria.

She spread bacteria over agar jelly in a Petri dish and added three discs that had each been soaked in a different antibiotic. She labelled the antibiotics A, B and C (see Figure 6.9a).

She left the dish in a warm place. Figure 6.9b shows the dish after 24 hours.

a 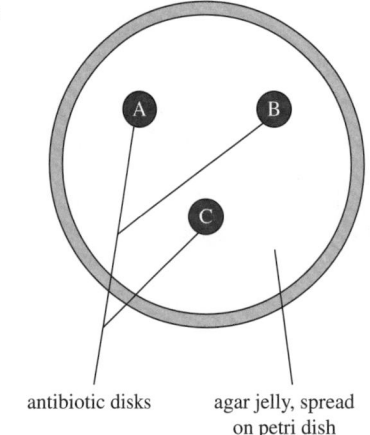   **b**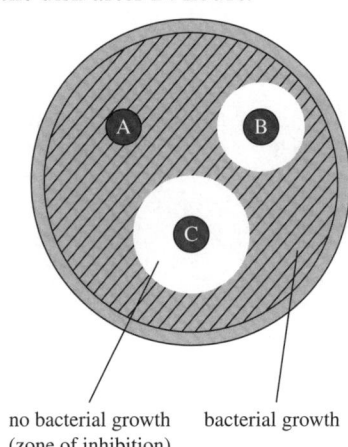

antibiotic disks   agar jelly, spread on petri dish   no bacterial growth (zone of inhibition)   bacterial growth

Figure 6.9a The dish before bacterial growth; **b** the dish after growth

She wanted to measure the area of the zone of inhibition around disc B.

These are the steps to take:

Step 1: Use a ruler to measure the radius of the circle.

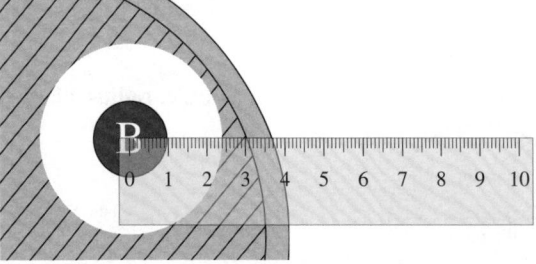

The radius is 2.4 cm.

Step 2: Square the radius (multiply it by itself).

$$2.4 \times 2.4 = 5.76$$

Step 3: Multiply the radius by π. Find this on your calculator.

$$5.76 \times \pi = 18.1$$

Step 4: Use the correct unit for the area.

$18.1 \, cm^2$

TIP

You can also calculate the radius by dividing the diameter in half.

Practice question 5

The radius of the zone of inhibition around disc C in Figure 6.9b is 4.4 cm.

Use the formula $A = \pi r^2$ to calculate the area of the zone of inhibition.

....

Practice question 6

The diameter of a Petri dish is 90 mm.

Use the formula $A = \pi r^2$ to calculate the area of the Petri dish in centimetres.

Give your answer to three significant figures.

....

....

LINK

See Chapter 1, 'Representing values', for more about significant figures.

Further question (Extention)

A scientist estimated the number of grass plants in an area of scrubland.

a   The diagram shows the square quadrat she used.

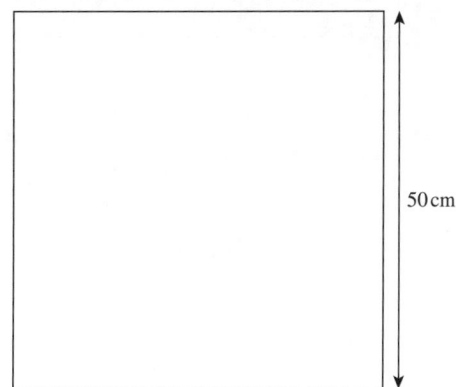

50 cm

Calculate its area in m².

....

....

b The diagram below shows an overhead view of the scrubland.

Use the grid to estimate its area.

....

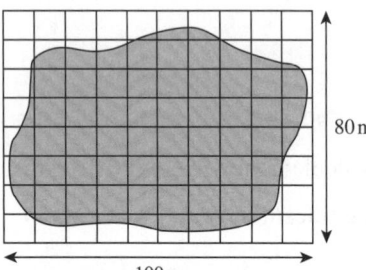

100 m

80 m

c The scientist placed the quadrat at 100 randomly chosen locations on the scrubland.

The mean number of grass plants within the quadrat was 1.7.

Use this to calculate an estimate for the number of grass plants in the entire area of scrubland.

....

....

Additional questions involving several maths skills

All exam-style questions and sample answers in this title were written by the authors.
In examinations, the way marks are awarded may be different.

1 A student investigated how temperature affects the rate of diffusion.

The diagram shows the equipment he used.

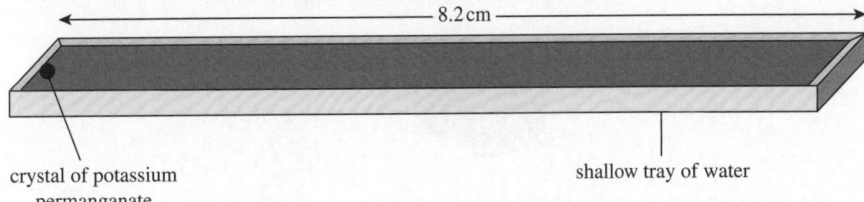

crystal of potassium
permanganate

shallow tray of water

He filled the tray with water at cold water and measured the time it took for colour from
the potassium permanganate to reach the end of the tray. It took 122 seconds.

He then repeated this with warm and then hot water.

The bar chart shows the results.

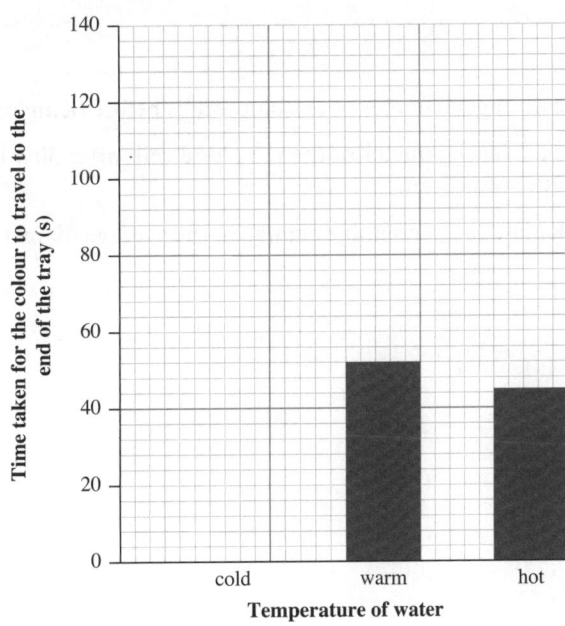

a Draw the bar for cold water.

b State how long it took for the colour to travel to the end in the warm water.

....

c Calculate the rate of movement for the colour in hot water. Give your answer in mm/s
to two significant figures.

....

....

d The student's teacher asked him to change his method so he could draw a line graph.

Describe how he should do this.

....

2   A scientist viewed red blood cells under the microscope and measured their diameter.

The average diameter of a red blood cell was 8 μm.

a   Convert this measurement into mm.

....

She then placed the red blood cells into sodium chloride solution.

The photo shows a microscope image of the red blood cells after 30 minutes.

The magnification used was × 4000.

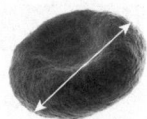

b   Calculate the diameter of the red blood cell labelled X.

Use the formula:

$$\text{real size} = \frac{\text{size of the image}}{\text{magnification}}$$

....

....

c   The average diameter of the blood cells before being placed in the solution was 8 μm.

The average diameter of the red blood cells after 30 minutes in the sodium chloride solution was 6 μm.

Calculate the percentage change in the average diameter of the red blood cells.

....

....

Glossary

accuracy How close a value is to the true value

anomalous result One of a series of repeated experimental results that is much larger or smaller than the others

area A measure of the size of a surface (measured in square units, for example, cm^2 or m^2)

axis A reference line on a graph or chart, along which a distance scale represents values of a variable

bar chart A chart with separated rectangular bars of equal width; the height (or length) of a bar represents the value of the variable

best-fit line A straight line or a smooth curve drawn on a graph that passes through or close to as many as possible of the data points; it represents the best estimate of the relationship between the variables

categorical data Data that can be grouped into categories (types) but not ordered

circumference The distance around a circle

class Group of ordered data in a frequency table or on a histogram

continuous data Data that can take any numerical value within a range

control variable Variable that is kept constant in an investigation

coordinates Values that determine the position of a data point on a graph, relative to the axes

correlation A measure of the closeness of the relationship between two variables; it may be *positive* (one variable increases when the other increases) or *negative* (one variable decreases when the other increases)

decimal place The place-value position of a number after a decimal point; the number 6.357 has three decimal places

dependent variable The variable that is measured or observed in an investigation, when the independent variable is changed

diameter A straight line connecting two points on a circle (or sphere) that passes through the centre

directly proportional The relationship between two variables such that when one doubles, the other doubles; the graph of the two variables is a straight line through the origin

discrete data Data that can take only certain values

distribution The way in which values in a data set are spread between the lowest and highest values

estimate (Find) an approximate value

extrapolation Extending the line of best fit on a graph beyond the range of the data, in order to estimate values not within the data set

frequency The number of times an event occurs or number of objects/people with a certain characteristic

frequency table A table showing the frequency of occurrence of certain categories or classes of data

gradient The slope (steepness) of a line on a graph; it is calculated by dividing the vertical change by the horizontal change

histogram A chart with bars showing the distribution of data that is grouped into classes; if the class intervals are equal, the height of a bar is proportional to the frequency of the class

independent variable Variable in an investigation that is changed by the experimenter

index A small number that indicates the power; for example, the index 4 here shows that the 2 is raised to the power 4, which means four 2s multiplied together: $2^4 = 2 \times 2 \times 2 \times 2$

intercept The point at which a line on a graph crosses one of the axes; usually refers to the intercept with the vertical (y-) axis

interpolation On a graph, to estimate the value of a variable from the value of the other variable, using a best-fit line; on a scale, to estimate a measurement that falls between two scale marks

line graph A graph of one variable against another where the data points fall on or close to a single line, which may be straight, curved or straight-line segments between points, depending on the relationship between the variables

linear relationship A relationship between two variables that can be represented on a graph by a straight line

magnification The factor by which something has been enlarged: $\text{magnification} = \dfrac{\text{length of image}}{\text{actual length}}$

mean An average value: the sum of a set of values divided by the number of values in the set

meniscus The curved surface of a liquid in a tube or cylinder

negative relationship When one variable decreases as the other increases

order of magnitude Approximate size of a number, often given as a power of 10; for example, the order of magnitude of 2700 is 10^3

origin The point on a graph at which the value of both variables is zero and where the axes cross

outlier A value in a data set, or point on a graph, that is considered unusual compared with the trend of other values

percentage A fraction expressed out of 100,

e.g. $\dfrac{1}{2} = \dfrac{50}{100} = 50\%$

pie chart A circular chart that is divided into sectors which represent the relative values of components: the angle of the sector is proportional to the value of the component

positive relationship When one variable increases as the other increases

power A number raised to the power 2 is squared (e.g. x^2); a number raised to the power 3 is cubed (e.g. x^3); and so on

power of ten A number such as 10^3 or 10^{-3}

precision The closeness of agreement between several measured values obtained by repeated measurements; the precision of a single value can be indicated by the number of significant figures given in the number, for example 4.027 has greater precision (is more precise) than 4.0

processed data Data produced by calculation using raw experimental data

qualitative data Data that are descriptive and not numerical

quantitative data Data that are numerical

radius The distance from the centre of a circle (or sphere) to the circle (or sphere surface)

random error Measurement error that varies in an unpredictable way from one measurement to the next

range The interval between a lowest value and a highest value, for example of a measured variable or on the scale of a measuring instrument

rate A measure of how much one variable changes relative to another variable; usually how quickly a variable changes as time progresses

ratio A comparison of two numbers or of two measurements with the same unit; the ratio of A to B can be written $A:B$ or expressed as a fraction $\dfrac{A}{B}$

resolution The smallest change in a value that can be observed on a measuring instrument

rounding Expressing a number as an approximation, with fewer significant figures, for example, 7.436 rounded to two significant figure is 7.4, or rounded to three significant figures it is 7.44

scale A set of marks with equal intervals, for example on a graph axis or a measuring cylinder; or, on a scale diagram, the ratio of a length in the diagram to the actual size

scale drawing A diagram in which all lengths are in the same ratio to the corresponding lengths in the actual object (to the same scale)

scale factor The ratio of a length in a scale drawing to the corresponding length in the actual object

scatter graph A graph of one variable against another which may or may not show a correlation between the two variables

scientific notation Another term for **standard form**

significant figures The number of digits in a number, not including any zeros at the beginning; for example, the number of significant figures in 0.0682 is three

standard form Notation in which a number is written as a number between 1 and 10 multiplied by a power of 10; for example, 4.78×10^9 ; also called **scientific notation** or **standard index form**

standard index form Another term for **standard form**

standard notation The form in which a number is normally written

surface area The total area of surface of a three-dimensional object

systematic error Measurement error that results in measured values differing from the true value by the same amount each time a measurement is made. This may occur, for example, when a balance reads 0.02 g with no mass on it

trend A pattern shown by data; on a graph this may be shown by points following a 'trend line', the best estimate of this being the best-fit line

uncertainty Range of variation in experimental results because of sources of error; the true value is expected to be within this range

unit A standard used in measuring a variable, for example the metre or the volt

unit prefix A prefix (term added to the front of a word) added to a unit name to indicate a power of 10 of that unit, e.g. 1 *millimetre* = 10^{-3} metre

volume A measure of three-dimensional space (measured in cubic units, e.g. cm^3 or m^3)

Acknowledgements

The authors and publishers acknowledge the following sources of copyright material and are grateful for the permissions granted.

Thanks to the following for permission to reproduce images:

Cover Frans Lanting/Science Photo Library; *Inside* GlobalP/GI; Lisegagne/GI; Michel Gunther/GI; GlobalP/GI; Science Picture Co/GI; Ed Reschke/GI; Ttsz/GI; Biophoto Associates/Science Photo Library; Ed Reschke/GI; Ttsz/GI; Greenwales/Alamy Stock Photo; Smith Collection/Gado/GI.

Key: GI = Getty Images